THE
CAIRO REVIEW
OF GLOBAL AFFAIRS

1 / Spring 2011

CONTENTS

BOOKS

Contributors

Jennifer Bremer is an associate professor of public policy and chair of the Public Policy and Administration Department at the American University in Cairo. Previously, she served as director of the Washington center of the Kenan Institute of Private Enterprise, a unit of the University of North Carolina, and as an international development consultant with Nathan Associates and Development Alternatives.

Nabil Fahmy is the founding dean of the School of Global Affairs and Public Policy at the American University in Cairo. A career diplomat, he served as Egypt's ambassador to the United States from 1999 to 2008, and as envoy to Japan between 1997 and 1999. He fulfilled many other roles in his country's foreign service, as a member of Egypt's mission to the United Nations in New York, and as a senior government advisor on nuclear disarmament. He has specialized in multilateral affairs, conflict resolution, and disarmament and has published frequently on these topics. He serves as the non-resident chair of the Middle East Nonproliferation Project of the James Martin Center for Nonproliferation Studies.

Shadi Hamid is director of research at the Brookings Doha Center and a fellow at the Saban Center for Middle East Policy at the Brookings Institution. He is a New Ideas Fund fellow for 2010–11, leading a project in Egypt, Jordan, and Morocco on U.S. democracy promotion strategies in the Arab world. He was previously director of research at the Project on Middle East Democracy and a Hewlett Fellow at Stanford University's Center on Democracy, Development, and the Rule of Law. He has also served as a program specialist on public diplomacy at the U.S. State Department and a legislative fellow in the office of Senator Diane Feinstein. Hamid is a frequent commentator on Middle East affairs and can be followed on Twitter at http://twitter.com/shadihamid.

Princeton N. Lyman is the United States Special Envoy for Sudan. Prior to his appointment to the post on March 31 by President Barack Obama, he served as director of the U.S. team for north–south negotiations in the special envoy's office. During his long career at the U.S. State Department, he served as ambassador to Nigeria and to South Africa, as assistant secretary of state for international organization affairs, and as deputy assistant secretary of state for African affairs.

Hafez Al Mirazi is director of the Kamal Adham Center for Journalism Training and Research at the American University in Cairo. He is also host of *Studio Cairo*, a weekly program about Egyptian politics featured on the Al-Arabiya satellite channel. Prior to returning to his native Egypt, Al Mirazi worked as a correspondent in the United States for nearly twenty-five years. He served as Washington bureau chief for Al Jazeera, and hosted the channel's weekly show *From Washington*.

William B. Quandt is Edward R. Stettinius Professor of Politics at the University of Virginia. He has taught at the University of California, Los Angeles, the Massachusetts Institute of Technology, and the University of Pennsylvania and was a senior fellow at the Brookings Institution. During the Nixon and Carter administrations, he served on the National Security Council; he played an active role in the negotiations that led to the Camp David accords and the Egyptian–Israeli peace treaty. He is the author of numerous books, including *Peace Process: American Diplomacy and the Arab–Israeli Conflict since 1967*, and *Camp David: Peacemaking and Politics*. Quandt is a member of the Board of Trustees of the American University in Cairo.

Joshua Cooper Ramo is the managing director of Kissinger Associates, an international consulting firm based in New York. His most recent book is *The Age of the Unthinkable: Why the New World Disorder Constantly Surprises Us and What We Can Do about It*. In an influential paper called "The Beijing Consensus" in 2004, published by the Foreign Policy Centre in Britain, he described the Chinese model of economic development and its attraction for developing nations. Ramo is a member of the World Economic Forum's Young Global Leaders, and is a former assistant managing editor and world section editor of *TIME*.

Shibley Telhami is the Anwar Sadat Professor for Peace and Development at the University of Maryland and a non-resident senior fellow at the Saban Center at the Brookings Institution. He has authored or edited numerous books, including *The Stakes: America and the Middle East*, *Power and Leadership in International Bargaining: The Path to the Camp David Accords*, *International Organizations and Ethnic Conflict*, and *Identity and Foreign Policy in the Middle East*. He was a member of the U.S. Advisory Group on Public Diplomacy in the Arab and Muslim World and served on the Iraq Study Group. He is a member of the Council on Foreign Relations and serves on the board of the Education for Employment Foundation.

Ahmed Zewail is the Linus Pauling Chair Professor of Chemistry and professor of physics at the California Institute of Technology. He also serves on President Barack Obama's Council of Advisors on Science and Technology, and is the U.S. Science Envoy to the Middle East. Zewail received the 1999 Nobel Prize in Chemistry for his pioneering work in the field of femtoscience. He has received many other distinguished awards, including the Grand Collar of the Nile, Egypt's highest state honor. Zewail, who was born in Egypt, is featured as the fourth Giza pyramid on an Egyptian postage stamp.

THE
CAIRO REVIEW
OF GLOBAL AFFAIRS www.thecairoreview.com

The Cairo Review of Global Affairs
School of Global Affairs and Public Policy
The American University in Cairo
Plaza 050, Abdul Latif Jameel Hall
AUC Avenue, PO Box 74
New Cairo 11835, Egypt
Tel. (20) 2 2615 3437
Email: editor@thecairoreview.com

Submissions:
Unsolicited manuscripts and article proposals are welcome. They can be sent to the Managing Editor by post or via email at editor@thecairoreview.com

Subscriptions:
Annual subscriptions are offered for $100 inclusive of shipping. Please send a check or money order in the amount of $100 to either of the following addresses:

The American University in Cairo Press
113 Kasr el Aini Street, P.O. Box 2511
Cairo 11511, Egypt

North American orders:
The American University in Cairo Press
420 Fifth Avenue
New York, NY 10018-2729, U.S.A.

The Cairo Review of Global Affairs is the quarterly journal of the School of Global Affairs and Public Policy at the American University in Cairo, published by the American University in Cairo Press.
ISSN: 2090-4819. Dar el Kutub No. 20533/10. ISBN: 978-977-416-463-7.
Designed by Andrea El-Akshar. Printed in the United States of America.

Note from the Dean

Ethar El-Katatney is an Egyptian born in Saudi Arabia. Troy Carter is an American from Montana. Besides being students at the American University in Cairo, they have something else in common. As reporter-researchers, they have been part of an editorial team launching the *Cairo Review of Global Affairs*.

This new quarterly journal, produced by AUC's School of Global Affairs and Public Policy, is intended to be an outlet for people in the Middle East who follow global affairs. We also want it to be a platform that gives perspectives from the region a greater voice in international policy conversations and debates. Creating a new publication—and we're in print, as well as online at www.thecairoreview.com—naturally requires a great effort. As Ethar and Troy can tell you, it's not made any easier when a revolution erupts on your doorstep as you are going to press with your inaugural issue. Our editorial team, headed by Managing Editor Scott MacLeod, a former *TIME* magazine correspondent and now a GAPP professor, struggled to keep production on track as Internet and phone services were shut down and a curfew went into effect. The bigger challenge was quickly revamping the contents of our first issue to reflect the monumental changes occurring in Egypt and throughout the region. To provide you with an inside perspective on the Arab revolution, the *Cairo Review* presents a gallery of interviews with leading political figures, policymakers, and analysts. In addition, Shadi Hamid of the Brookings Institution provides an overview of the struggle for democracy in the Middle East. And we are especially proud to publish an article by Ahmed Zewail, the Nobel laureate from Egypt, on the urgent need to reform Arab education as the region advances into a new era.

We sought expertise from around the world in creating the *Cairo Review*, but didn't have to look far for some members of our editorial team. Ethar took a graduate course in digital media taught by MacLeod last year before she headed to China to produce a series of articles on Islam in that country; Troy, who formerly served with U.S. forces in Iraq and Afghanistan, walked into the *Cairo Review*'s offices after hearing about the new journal from a professor. Besides their work for us, Ethar and Troy have logged countless hours in Tahrir Square as journalists covering the history being made there.

As our staff illustrates, it's surely a global world out there. We hope you enjoy reading the *Cairo Review of Global Affairs*.

Nabil Fahmy
Dean, School of Global Affairs and Public Policy

A University and a Revolution

Lara El-Gibaly, a junior at the American University in Cairo, eagerly anticipated the start of the Spring Semester. A nineteen-year-old journalism major, she was preparing to take the helm as editor in chief of AUC's student newspaper, the *Caravan*. During the winter break, she had an internship at the Cairo Bureau of Al Jazeera, the Qatar-based satellite television news network. Instead of performing mundane chores like shuffling through incoming faxes, however, she suddenly found herself doing something quite extraordinary: covering a revolution.

No journalism class could have prepared her for what happened next. As the mass uprising got underway in Tahrir Square, El-Gibaly choked back the effects of tear gas that enveloped protesters emerging from a nearby mosque in defiance of baton-wielding police. In the days that followed, she served as a field producer for profiles of youth activists and a story on a fourteen-year-old boy shot to death while out buying bread. At one point, she and other Al Jazeera personnel went into hiding after state security operatives moved in to shut down the Al Jazeera bureau. "We had to put on disguises and leave the hotel with crazy exit plans, things I imagined only happen in movies," she recalls.

> "I like to be the change I want to see."
> —Gigi Ibrahim

As the revolution tugged at El-Gibaly's patriotic heartstrings, she remained determined to fulfill her professional responsibilities. "There were times I wanted to participate in the infectious chants," she says. "I'd be tapping my foot and snapping my fingers to the beat, but I had to tell myself what I was doing was contributing just as much to the revolution—getting the truth out there."

El-Gibaly was one of countless AUC students, professors, staff members, and alumni who participated in one way or another in Egypt's remarkable eighteen-day revolution in January and February. At times, the downtown campus directly on Tahrir Square became a battleground; without the university's consent, security forces used rooftops to fire on demonstrators below. Wael Ghonim, a Google executive who earned

oriental Hall, etc.

When Egypt's popular uprising began on January 25, the American University in Cairo became part of the historic events. The gates of the ninety-two-year-old downtown campus open directly onto Tahrir Square, the focal point of the mass protests. Following the resumption of classes in February after a two-week interruption, the university remained absorbed with everything connected with the revolution. The Egyptian public and AUC students alike crammed lecture halls to hear debates about the country's future, and to attend a documentary film program, ***Egypt Rising***. Workshops and teach-ins on everything from rhetoric and ethics to civil society empowerment multiplied across the old campus and the new campus in the suburb of New Cairo. Middle East experts like **Rashid Khalidi** of Columbia University and **Shibley Telhami** of the University of Maryland visited to talk on the broader meaning of the uprising. Among the courses quickly developed around the revolution theme: ***"Isqat Al-Nizam*: Egypt's 25 January Uprising in Comparative Historical Perspective,"** coordinated by **Michael Reimer** of the history department.

AUC is also archiving the events through such projects as **"University on the Square: Documenting Egypt's 21st-Century Revolution."** Intended for historians, activists, students, and the general public, the results will be on display in AUC's **Rare Books Library** as well as in future public exhibitions, publications, seminars, and on AUC's website. Part of the project involves obtaining oral histories from AUC students, faculty, staff, and alumni who lived through the momentous days. Besides undergrads out in the square protesting, AUC security personnel who guarded the Tahrir campus through perilous days and nights are among those interviewed for their personal accounts. Another aspect of the project is assembling a collection of revolution artifacts, including photographs and some of the ubiquitous Egyptian flags waved by the demonstrators. AUC intern **Sean Graham** helped launch the effort by scavenging Tahrir Square for leftover homemade protest signs, bullet casings, and tear gas canisters, which he initially stashed in his dorm room. Another item being eyed for the artifacts collection awaits a permanent display venue: a burned out car found near the campus. Says Graham: "This is a remarkable period in Egypt's history. This is also a part of my history. The project gives us a chance to share that history with others, to tell our collective story for generations to come."

◆ Madeline B. Welsh

an MBA from AUC in 2007, became a symbol of the revolution after organizing the protests via Facebook and being detained for twelve days. He shot to international prominence after giving an emotional interview about his role to Egyptian television presenter Mona El-Shazly, another AUC graduate.

El-Gibaly's friend and classmate, Sarah Abdelrahman, twenty-three, also found unexpected fame—she appeared with other students on the cover of *TIME* magazine, illustrating a story about a generation changing the world. A drama student more accustomed to memorizing lines than dodging tear gas canisters, she quickly took to the streets and started learning how to make Molotov cocktails.

Abdelrahman relates a tale of personal change that is echoed by many young Egyptian revolutionaries. She recalls that on the eve of the protests, she had voiced her decision to leave Egypt upon graduation, to pursue studies and possibly her entire future abroad. Filled with national pride amid the revolution, however, she changed her birthdate on her Facebook page to January 25 to symbolize her rebirth as an Egyptian citizen. "Fear controlled us, but not anymore," she explains. "I suddenly have a sense of ownership in this country and I have a sense of purpose. I need to rebuild Egypt. That's what I want to spend my life doing."

Gigi Ibrahim, twenty-four, made such a commitment after graduating from AUC in 2010. A self-styled activist and citizen journalist, recognizable by her Palestinian *keffiyeh*, she organized labor strikes at the university prior to the revolution. Living in Tahrir Square for the eighteen days of protests, she amassed ten thousand followers on Twitter, spoke as an expert commentator on international news networks, and became a subject in the PBS Frontline documentary *Revolution in Cairo*, aired in late February. "The celebrity factor is a little weird," Ibrahim says. "This is something I have always done and will continue to do, whether I have media attention or not. Usually people just complain about problems. They take a stand but just watch. I like to lead by example and be the change I want to see."

In common with many AUC students and recent graduates, Ibrahim is experiencing a dual transformation—as an Egyptian citizen in the revolution, and as a daughter in her Egyptian family. "I struggled every day with my family, especially my dad, who didn't believe in what I did," recalls Ibrahim, who earned a degree in political science. She is pleased to report success on both fronts. "They now support me," she says. "That's a huge relief and victory. I feel blessed and humble and lucky to have witnessed and taken part."

◆ Lauren E. Bohn

Lisa Anderson's world view

Upon entering the office of the American University in Cairo President Lisa Anderson, you'll admire the beautiful colored globe prominently displayed on a table. But dozens of globes? There's a collection of smaller globes on a bookshelf. There are bowls of tiny globes (key chains, actually) on a coffee table. Globes, globes, everywhere.

The globes capture some of the zeitgeist around AUC. Anderson brought them from her former office at Columbia University, where she served as dean of the School of International and Public Affairs. But their display in Cairo isn't merely the standard décor for a political scientist, but Anderson's idea of a subtle provocation. AUC, founded by American Christians in 1919, is commonly seen as a cultural bridge: between the United States and Egypt, and between the West and the Arab and Muslim worlds. As true and important as that may be, Anderson insists on highlighting AUC's global vision and role. "We're not just about East and West," she says. "Because of our tradition with America, we privilege the U.S., of course. But that's not all there is in the world. Don't forget China, and India, and Brazil. We are just as much a window on what's going on in Singapore and Japan as we are on what's going on in the United States."

"we're not just about east and west."

Not to mention, of course, a window on what's going on in Egypt. Anderson along with everyone at AUC literally had a front row seat to history when young Egyptians launched a popular uprising on January 25 and toppled the thirty-year regime of President Hosni Mubarak eighteen dramatic days later. Many current and former students took part in the protests centered on Cairo's Tahrir Square, site of AUC's older, downtown campus. "Difficult as these days have been—and there may be more trials to come—all of us should be proud," says Anderson, a Middle East specialist. "It is an honor and privilege to be witness to fruits of a generation's investment in their children." In her first month as AUC's eleventh president and first woman to hold the position–she served as AUC provost from 2008 to 2010–Anderson thus contended with security forces and demonstrators using the campus as a battleground and held town hall meetings with faculty and students across the city. With the revolution still in full swing, she presided over AUC planning to recognize its achievements, commemorate those who died, assist Egypt's transition to democracy and launch new research projects.

In Anderson's view, AUC's robust engagement with the historic transformation in Egypt and the Arab world will be another contribution to the university's goal of becoming a global leader in education and research. David D. Arnold, president from 2003–10 and now head of the Asia Foundation headquartered in San Francisco, set the stage by constructing AUC's new $400 million, 260-acre, state-of-the-art main campus in the eastern suburb of New Cairo. AUC has recently undertaken significant academic initiatives as well, such as the establishment of the new School of Global Affairs and Public Policy, and building partnerships with counterparts like Harvard University in the U.S., Oxford University and Cambridge University in the United Kingdom, and the King Abdullah University of Science and Technology in Saudi Arabia. AUC's enrollment has grown from five thousand to more than six thousand students, including one thousand in the graduate programs.

Now under Anderson's stewardship, AUC's aim is to bolster its research capabilities through strategic investments, and thereby secure a ranking place in the emerging new paradigm of global education. Along with her successor as provost Medhat Haroun, Anderson shepherded the establishment of the first PhD program in the university's ninety-two-year history—in the School of Sciences and Engineering—and believes that one of her mandates as president is to inspire AUC's other five schools to follow suit. "Global reputations are made by graduate programs," she explains. "You can bring in more research dollars and collaborations if you have graduate programs. We will be thinking of how we can build out our PhD programs without sacrificing the excellence of our undergraduate liberal arts mission."

Anderson argues that AUC is well positioned to become a node in one of the networks of global research universities she believes are beginning to come into focus. "Within the next ten to twenty years, you'll see the appearance of a set of institutions that are globally connected," she says. "They will have networks of collaborations, of student exchanges, and faculty appointments. You'll see some of the perfectly fine institutions in the U.S. fading because they can't sustain a global reach, in favor of institutions in various other parts of the world. You can begin to see the privileging of what we used to call the periphery."

"within the next ten to twenty years, you'll see the appearance of a set of institutions that are globally connected . . ."

Without a doubt, Anderson believes, aspirants for leading places in the evolving networks will have a significant advantage if they are located in "fabulous global cities"—for instance, fabulous global cities like Cairo. "As one of the provosts of Columbia used to say, New York City is its shadow endowment—faculty and students want to come to Columbia because it is in New York," Anderson says. "AUC has Cairo, both in its name and as a resource. The city is an integral part of the curriculum. People come to AUC because of where it is."

In 1976, Anderson herself was one of those young students who trekked to AUC—to study Arabic for a summer. She would go on to receive her PhD in political science from Columbia in 1981, and to a career as a professor at Harvard and professor and then dean at Columbia. She has served as director of Columbia's Middle East Institute, and is a past president of the Middle East Studies Association and former chair of the board of directors of the Social Science Research Council. She recalls, however, that her lifelong attachment to the Middle East and scholarly focus on North Africa began as an undergraduate at Sarah Lawrence College when a professor assigned a research paper on Egypt. "I wrote eighty pages on the history of Egypt from Mohammed Ali to Nasser and just loved it," she says. "As a result, I abandoned my aspirations to become a civil rights lawyer. I told myself I would study this region until I was tired of it." She adds, "As you can tell, I have never gotten tired of it."

Besides introducing Anderson to the Middle East, the professor also instilled in her a sense that education can change the world. The daughter of liberal parents who opposed the Vietnam War, Anderson went home during a school break as a supporter of the war after the professor forced her to question her unexamined assumptions. "I eventually ended up back in my parents' camp," she says. "But that professor taught me the power of critical thinking, that if you only believe in something because your parents told you, you need to question it." That dynamic was evident, she points out, when so many young Egyptians decided to abandon the fearful conservatism of their parents' generation and take to the streets on January 25. "A new generation has come of age that can be agile and imaginative and able to confront the problems–many of which we still cannot imagine–that it will inevitably face," she says.

For Anderson, those challenges are less about a clash between the West and the Muslim world than they are about reconciling global and local interests. Returning to live and work in Cairo less than a decade after the September 11, 2001, attack on New York, Anderson says she's been struck by how compelling other issues seem to be. "No doubt, in the U.S. there's a lot of anxiety about the region, and in the region there's a lot of anxiety about America," she explains. "But some of this is manufactured on both sides, because people make reputations and money from it. I don't think it's the most interesting challenge of the future. If you think about the role that institutions like ours should be playing, I think it is in linking the local and the global. Some of this political tension is due to that struggle rather than a clash of civilizations."

That brings Anderson back to perceptions of the "American" in AUC's name. She prefers to emphasize AUC's deep roots throughout Egyptian society and its growing international role, rather than the conventional view of AUC as an American outpost in Egypt and the region. "Honestly," she exclaims, "that's a little passé now. East and West is a twentieth-century way of looking at the world. Now we need to be thinking about what's going to happen in the next twenty-five years on a global level, and about what role Egypt and the region will play there."

◆ Lauren E. Bohn

Training Arab policy Makers

Due to its geography and political standing, Egypt has interacted with the wider world throughout its long history. In taking its place on the international stage, it has produced honored statesmen and Nobel laureates. It has provided numerous global public servants, including a secretary general of the United Nations and a director general of the International Atomic Energy Agency.

With such a legacy in mind, and with a wary eye on the complex challenges facing Egypt and the Middle East, the American University in Cairo last year established the School of Global Affairs and Public Policy (GAPP) as the first institution of its kind in the region. GAPP's mission is to prepare students to join the next generation of policy makers and policy shapers, by providing them with the multidisciplinary skills and global perspectives available in the school's eight academic departments and research centers.

At GAPP's inauguration, Dean Nabil Fahmy addressed the gravity of the policy challenges ahead when he contrasted human achievements like space exploration and disease eradication with human failures such as widespread poverty and nuclear proliferation.

"Passivism and apathy are not options or choices that we can afford or condone," Fahmy warned. "Nor can the world community respond appropriately if it does not empower itself. It is time here and now to embrace the policies that will allow our collective genius to substitute and contain the avaricious greed that has often put us on the road toward self-destruction." With the establishment of GAPP, he concluded, "We are determined to make a difference."

Fahmy's appointment as founding dean perhaps represents the imperative of educating future practitioners as well as theorists. He himself attended AUC, earning a Bachelor of Science degree in physics and mathematics in 1974 and a Master of Arts degree in management in 1976. Initially inclined to enter international banking after graduation, he turned to public service instead. He took up his current academic post coming from a distinguished career in Egypt's foreign ministry, having served most recently as ambassador to the United States between 1999 and 2008 and as Egyptian envoy to Japan before that. In his numerous diplomatic assignments, including positions with Egypt's United Nations mission, he often focused on security and arms control issues. He is the nonresident chair of the Middle East Nonproliferation Project of the James Martin Center for Nonproliferation Studies at the Monterey Institute of International Studies.

In taking on its mission, GAPP brings together the resources of three existing departments (Journalism and Mass Communication, Public Policy and Administration, and Law) and five research centers (the Cynthia Nelson Institute for Gender and Women Studies, the Center for Migration and Refugee Studies, the Kamal Adham Center for Journalism Training and Research, the Middle East Studies Center, and the Prince Alwaleed bin Talal bin Abdulaziz al-Saud Center for American Studies and Research). Together, these offer students a rich mix of policy studies.

The school's formation did not alter core curricula, but its departments and research centers were directed to instill seven fundamental competencies in their existing programs: critical analytical skills, public policy orientation, a global perspective, multi- and interdisciplinary experience, quality research skills, professional experience, and effective communication skills.

With its dynamic approach and global perspective, GAPP is intent on establishing strategic partnerships with other institutions around the world. These already include ties with the Dubai School of Government (United Arab Emirates); the National Graduate Institute for Policy Studies (Japan); the Lee Kuan Yew School of Public Policy (Singapore); the Elliott School of International Affairs and the Trachtenberg School of Public Policy and Public Administration (both at George Washington University), and the Monterey Institute of International Studies (Middlebury College) in the U.S.; the Danish School of Media and Journalism (Århus, Denmark); and the Central Agency for Organization and Administration in Egypt.

A vital part of GAPP's mission is its Executive Education Program, which is providing specialized management, communications, and analytical training for public officials in Egypt and throughout the region.

To further promote a public role, and to raise students' awareness of public policy

"passivism and apathy are not options or choices that we can afford or condone. we are determined to make a difference."

—Nabil Fahmy

issues, Fahmy has undertaken several other initiatives as well. One of them is the creation of the *Cairo Review of Global Affairs*, GAPP's quarterly policy journal.

Another is the launch of the Public Policy Lecture Series, which enables AUC students and Egyptians at large to hear the views of local and international figures from various fields. The series has played an especially important role since Egypt's January 25 revolution. In public seminars at the AUC downtown campus, steps away from Tahrir Square, GAPP has brought together legal experts and leading politicians to debate critical issues facing Egypt's transition to democracy, such as changes in the constitution and the formation of new political parties. The series kicked off last year with a speech on Turkish policy in the Middle East by Turkish Foreign Minister Ahmet Davutoglu, who attended AUC in the 1980s. Other earlier speakers in the series have included former UN undersecretary general Lakhdar Brahimi, French diplomat and author Eric Rouleau, and Academy Award-winning film director Costa Gavras.

In AUC's ninety-two-year history, it has awarded degrees to more than twenty-five thousand students, many of whom went on to make significant contributions to public service. AUC's establishment of the first school in the region dedicated to providing education and training in public policy comes at a particularly fitting moment, when political transformation is presenting the Middle East with new challenges and opportunities. "We are making the direct and invaluable link between theory and practice," says Associate Dean Laila El Baradei: "We want our students to have a real impact on the policies of tomorrow."

◆ Ross S. Donohue

Islam and Gender

It may seem counterintuitive for many to hear an icon of feminism defending the Muslim veil. But don't expect to receive conventional wisdom when you discuss issues such as the role of women in the Middle East with Judith Butler. She is the Maxine Elliot Professor in the Departments of Rhetoric and Comparative Literature at the University of California, Berkeley, and author of the acclaimed *Gender Trouble: Feminism and the Subversion of Identity*.

Butler believes that the veils worn by some Muslim women have unjustly become universal symbols of female disempowerment. For her, veiling is partly an expression of cultural belonging, signifying a variety of meanings that must be understood through different religions, cultures, and regions. Sometimes, she says, the veil also signifies a way of resisting compulsory assimilation to so-called 'Western' norms. "I think women around the world are now trying to figure out how they honor certain practices, religious traditions, and the communities where they belong," Butler explained over tea with the *Cairo Review* in November, before delivering the sixth Edward W. Said Memorial Lecture at the American University in Cairo. "What I think is misunderstood is that the veil signifies a mode of cultural belonging and values. There are, of course, many forms of agency through the veil."

At the same time, Butler believes, many Muslim women are trying to negotiate autonomy for themselves, to enter into the public sphere. "There's always some degree of anxiety and fear of punishment in departing from gender norms," she argues, as she has so often before about the difficulties inherent in those negotiations. "That's as true for an effeminate boy in Wyoming as it is for a woman in Cairo."

Butler is harsh on the tendency in the West, especially among feminists, to categorically condemn the veil. "Negotiating questions of sexuality and gender is not always done according to the same language you find in the U.S. or in France," she explains. "It's not always a rights discourse. It's a different kind of negotiation, but critics very often don't have the patience to learn about it. The idea of liberating Afghan women under the Bush presidency was to tear off the veil in front of the global media. But that comes very close to a new form of cultural possession: 'You now belong to the West. We get to consume your visual beauty as we wish.' We need to be a little more careful before we assume that the veil signifies the loss of autonomy."

"we need to be a little more careful before we assume that the veil signifies the loss of autonomy."

Adds Butler: "If we allow Islam or the problem of women in Islam to stand for contemporary problems of women's inequality, then I think we're scapegoating. We're not actually thinking more concretely about the many sources of relative inequality in the West, which include the sexual division of labor, the disproportionate number of women who suffer across the globe from poverty and illiteracy. We need to think about gender regulations in a global and comparative way so that some abstract idea of a woman with the veil does not become the signifier of sexual oppression. It really gets the so-called West off the hook and it displays extraordinary ignorance about the history and present of Muslim practices."

◆ Lauren E. Bohn

THE STRUGGLE FOR MIDDLE EAST DEMOCRACY

Why the Arab Street Finally Revolted

By Shadi Hamid

It always seemed as if Arab countries were 'on the brink.' It turns out that they were. And those who assured us that Arab autocracies would last for decades, if not longer, were wrong. In the wake of the Tunisian and Egyptian revolutions, academics, analysts and certainly Western policymakers must reassess their understanding of a region entering its democratic moment.

What has happened since January disproves longstanding assumptions about how democracies can—and should—emerge in the Arab world. Even the neo-conservatives, who seemed passionately attached to the notion of democratic revolution, told us this would be a generational struggle. Arabs were asked to be patient, and to wait. In order to move toward democracy, they would first have to build a secular middle class, reach a certain level of economic growth, and, somehow, foster a democratic culture. It was never quite explained how a democratic culture could emerge under dictatorship.

In the early 1990s, the United States began emphasizing civil society development in the Middle East. After the attacks of September 11, 2001, the George W. Bush administration significantly increased American assistance to the region. By fiscal year 2009, the level of annual U.S. democracy aid in the Middle East was more than the total amount spent between 1991 to 2001.[1]

But while it was categorized as democracy aid, it wasn't necessarily meant to promote democracy. Democracy entails 'alternation of power,' but most NGOs that received Western assistance avoided anything that could be construed as supporting a change in regime.

▷ Egyptians protesting in Tahrir Square, Cairo, Feb. 10, 2011. *Amel Pain/ EPA/Corbis*

The reason was simple. The U.S. and other Western powers supported 'reform,' but they were not interested in overturning an order which had given them pliant, if illegitimate, Arab regimes. Those regimes became part of a

comfortable strategic arrangement that secured Western interests in the region, including a forward military posture, access to energy resources and security for the state of Israel. Furthermore, the West feared that the alternative was a radical Islamist takeover reminiscent of the Iranian revolution of 1979.

The regimes themselves—including those in Egypt, Jordan, Morocco, Algeria, and Yemen—dutifully created the appearance of reform, rather than its substance. Democratization was 'defensive' and 'managed.' It was not meant to lead to democracy but rather to prevent its emergence. What resulted were autocracies always engaging in piecemeal reform but doing little to change the underlying power structure. Regime opponents found themselves ensnared in what political scientist Daniel Brumberg called an 'endless transition.'[2] This endless transition was always going to be a dangerous proposition, particularly in the long run. If a transition was promised and never came, Arabs were bound to grow impatient.

How, then, does change occur? The U.S. and European policy communities coalesced around the notion of 'gradualism.' Nearly everyone said they supported the objective of Arab democracy but few seemed to think that anything creative or bold should be done to bring it about. It made more sense to focus on economic reform first and political change later. Perhaps it was just a matter of being realistic, of accepting that politics—and, by extension, foreign policy—was the art of the possible. Revolution was impossible.

Hundreds of millions of dollars in Western assistance poured into the Arab world, assisting small NGOs, supporting often weak political parties, and empowering women to run for parliaments that had little power in the first place. This aid, while crucial for organizations with no source of indigenous funding, fell well short of what was required—a comprehensive, aggressive program supporting democratization.

There was something admirable about pro-democracy organizations like the National Endowment for Democracy and the National Democratic Institute working under difficult constraints, trying to push Arab regimes to open up, even if slightly. They were funded by successive U.S. administrations that were not, in fact, ready for actual democracy. Supporting civil society and offering training and technical assistance to secular political parties seemed like a workable compromise.

Colored Revolutions

During the Colored Revolutions, the West had played an altogether different role, offering critical support not just for change but regime change. In both the Rose Revolution in Georgia and the Orange Revolution in Ukraine, the trigger was stolen elections. Independent media played a key role in publicizing the fraud. The founder of Rustavi–2, one of Georgia's most watched channels and the voice of the opposition, had set up the station with the assistance of a USAID-funded nonprofit called Internews. On November 2, 2003, the day of the contested polls, and during the vote count, Rustavi–2 ran a scroll on the screen comparing the official results to the parallel vote count and exit polling, which was funded in part by Western governments and NGOs. Meanwhile, Pravda Ukraine, an important media outlet during the Orange Revolution, was operating out of Washington, DC and relied almost entirely on Western funding.

In Serbia, Otpor ('Resistance'), a student group, had been central in the overthrow of President Slobodan Milosevic in the year 2000. Otpor was directly funded by both the U.S. government and nongovernmental sources. USAID directly gave hundreds of thousands of dollars to the student group. Reportedly, a considerable amount was also channeled through covert American aid. Otpor's Ukrainian counterpart Pora ('High Time') also received direct funding from Western governments. Meanwhile, George Soros's Open Society Institute funded explicitly revolutionary activities. In the summer of 2003, OSI organized the visit of leading Otpor activists to train over one thousand young Georgians in nonviolent resistance.

Unlike the often impenetrable and calibrated language it used in addressing the Arab world, the West's rhetoric in Eastern Europe was clear and unapologetic. During Ukraine's second round of elections in November 2004, President George W. Bush sent Senator Richard Lugar as his special envoy. Lugar issued a forceful statement condemning President Leonid Kuchma's government for election fraud. Soon after, Secretary of State Colin Powell refused to recognize the election results and warned that "if the Ukrainian government does not act immediately and responsibly, there will be consequences for our relationship, for Ukraine's hopes for a Euro-Atlantic integration, and for individuals responsible for perpetrating fraud." As political scientist Michael McFaul recounts, the protestors in Maidan Square applauded when Powell's statement was read.[3] Meanwhile, Lech Walesa, Poland's first democratically elected president, assured the crowd that the West was on their side. The West had aligned itself with revolution.

The West and the Arab World

The Tunisian and Egyptian regimes fell faster than anyone could have expected. But it also took longer than anyone should have imagined. Where opposition groups in Eastern Europe came to count on Western support, in the Arab world, they often found themselves standing alone.

In September 2010, I asked a senior figure in Ayman Nour's Al-Ghad ('Tomorrow') party why liberal groups were having so much trouble gaining traction. "Everywhere else," he told me, "the reformers had the support of the international community.

We don't have that." Indeed, there had always been a pervasive sense among Arab opposition groups—especially in Egypt and Jordan, two of the largest recipients of U.S. aid—that they were fighting on two fronts, not only repressive regimes but their Western backers as well. Before the revolution, Ahmed Maher, a leader of Egypt's left-leaning April 6 Movement, put it this way: "The problem isn't with [President Hosni] Mubarak's policies. The problem is with American policy and what the American government wants Mubarak to do. His existence is totally in their hands."

It may have been the case that America's influence—and leverage with Arab autocrats—was on the decline. Perceptions, however, are more important than an objective assessment of U.S. capabilities. The Arab opposition attributed outsize importance to the West's ability to direct and determine its own fortunes. This sense of powerlessness fueled burgeoning Arab anger and frustration as well as widespread anti-Americanism. Perceived U.S. bias toward Israel was central, but so too was the general sense that the West had blocked, sometimes purposefully, the natural development of an entire people and region. That reality put Arab opposition groups in the awkward situation of seeing America as the hope for democracy but, at the same time, hating it for falling so short.

Similarly, Islamist leaders would often speak of an 'American veto' used by U.S. and European officials to block democratic outcomes not to their liking. As senior Muslim Brotherhood leader Essam El-Erian told me at the height of regime repression in 2008: "Even if you come to power through democratic means, you are facing an international community that doesn't accept the existence of the Islamist representation. This is a problem. I think this will continue to present an obstacle for us until there is a real acknowledgement of the situation."

In recent years, a growing academic literature and considerable empirical support have pointed to the critical role of international actors in bringing down autocrats. In their recent book, Steve Levitsky and Lucan Way provide extensive empirical support to what many have long argued. They write, "It was an externally driven shift in the cost of suppression, not changes in domestic conditions, that contributed most centrally to the demise of authoritarianism in the 1980s and 1990s." Levitsky and Way find that "states' vulnerability to Western democratization pressure . . . was often decisive."[4] The key word here is "often."

America's staunch support of repressive regimes, and its unwillingness to back pro-democracy movements, helps explain why the Arab world—until January 2011—seemed immune to democratic change. But it does not explain why, finally, Egyptians and Tunisians, with the odds stacked against them, found a way to defy expectations and even history, bringing about their own remarkable revolutions.

Arab Springs

In 2011, the Middle East witnessed the second 'Arab Spring'. The first—now somewhat forgotten—took place in 2005. President George W. Bush had announced in November 2003 a "forward strategy for freedom in the Middle East." In a speech to the National Endowment for Democracy, he declared: "Sixty years of Western nations excusing and accommodating the lack of freedom in the Middle East did nothing to make us safe—because in the long run, stability cannot be purchased at the expense of liberty."

The Bush administration cited democracy promotion among the reasons for its invading Iraq and toppling dictator Saddam Hussein in 2003. As dubious, cynical and inconsistent as they may have been, Bush's policies helped produce an otherwise unlikely outcome. The year 2005 saw the largest outpouring of pro-democracy activism the region had ever seen up until then. On January 31, 2005, Iraqis braved terrorist threats to cast meaningful ballots for the first time. In Bahrain, fifty thousand Bahrainis—one-eighth of the population—rallied for constitutional reform. And there was, of course, the Cedar Revolution, which led to a removal of Syrian troops from Lebanese territory. The Iraq war frightened Arab regimes into thinking that President Bush was serious about his democratizing mission.

However, after a succession of Islamist election victories in Egypt, Saudi Arabia, Lebanon, and the Palestinian territories, the U.S. backed off from its aggressive pro-democracy posture. With a deteriorating security situation in Iraq, a rising Iran, and a smoldering Israeli–Palestinian conflict, Arab democracy came to seem an unaffordable luxury. This was not a time for unsettling friendly Arab autocrats. Their Islamist competitors, known for their inflammatory anti-Americanism, were, at best, an unknown quantity. American policymakers shared an instinctive distrust of Islamists and made little effort to understand how they had changed. At worst, Americans feared, the Islamists would use their newfound power to roll back U.S. influence in the region.

Without America to worry about, regimes felt they could do as they pleased. Beginning in 2006, Egypt experienced the worst wave of anti-Islamist repression since the 1960s, while Jordan, long considered one of the more open, progressive Arab states, gradually descended into full-blown authoritarianism. Nearly every Arab country in the region experienced a decline in political rights and freedoms.

This was the Arab world that the newly elected President Barack Obama had to contend with. Instead of challenging the authoritarian status quo, Obama reluctantly accepted it. In his historic Cairo University address of June 2009, he promised a "new beginning." Instead, the Obama administration moved to rebuild relationships—frayed from Bush's democracy posturing—with Egyptian President Mubarak and other autocrats.

President Obama got one thing right—the centrality of the Israeli–Palestinian conflict to Arab grievance—but he got another wrong: that conflict was not, nor had it ever been, the most important problem facing the region. But pursuing peace seemed a more promising course than trying to refashion American foreign policy into a force for something—Arab democracy—it had actively resisted the previous five decades. The U.S. needed, or thought it needed, the support of 'moderate' Arab regimes to push the peace process forward. What Obama did, albeit unwittingly, was remove the U. S. from its central place in the ongoing Arab conversation over democracy. However hated he was, President Bush had injected himself into the regional debate. The struggle for Arab democracy had been internationalized.

Under President Obama, the U.S. increasingly seemed beside the point. The election of Obama—with his evident desire to build bridges with the Arab world, not to mention his Muslim family and middle name—was the best possible outcome that Arabs could have hoped for. It was difficult to think of an American politician who seemed as sympathetic and thoughtful about the challenges facing the region. But even the best possible outcome wasn't nearly enough. America's unwillingness to align itself with democratic forces was not, it seemed, a matter of one president over another, but a structural problem inherent in U.S. foreign policy.

The optimism over the Cairo speech quickly subsided. Somehow, in several Arab countries, U.S. favorability ratings dropped lower under President Obama than they were in the final years of the George W. Bush administration. The months leading up to the Egyptian and Tunisian revolutions were characterized by a renewed despair. The Mubarak regime had embarked on a systematic crackdown on opposition groups and independent media, culminating in perhaps the most rigged elections in the country's history. The results of the first round—returning 209 out of 211 seats to the ruling party—surprised everyone, including even regime officials hoping for a more 'credible' result.

I was in Egypt covering the elections. In the neighborhoods of Medinat Nasr and Shubra, I talked to the Muslim Brotherhood 'whips' (the representatives who count the votes). One by one, they ran me through all the violations. They didn't seem angry as much as resigned. But while opposition groups were demoralized, they, along with a growing number of Egyptians, began to realize, with much greater clarity, that gradual reform from within the system was impossible. The old paradigm—of pushing for small openings from within—was roundly discredited. Calls for civil disobedience and mass protest intensified. The ingredients were there—the anger, disillusion, and the loss of faith in a system made for and by ruling elites. All that was missing was a spark.

The First Arab Revolution

Before Tunisia, there were no successful examples of popular Arab revolutions. The closest a mass movement came to ousting a regime was in 1991, when the Islamic Salvation Front (FIS) won the Algerian elections in what was, up until then, the region's most promising democratic experiment and one of its earliest. With the tacit, and sometimes not so tacit, support of Europe and the United States, the military annulled the polls, banned the FIS, and sent thousands of Islamists to desert camps. "When you support democracy, you take what democracy gives you," U.S. Secretary of State James Baker explained later. "We didn't live with it in Algeria because we felt that the radical fundamentalists' views were so adverse to what we believe in and what we support, and to what we understood the national interests of the United States to be." The fear of Islamists in power paralyzed Western policymakers, turning a difficult situation into a destructive one. The civil war that soon broke out would claim the lives of an estimated one hundred thousand Algerians.

Having a model helps. In Eastern Europe, Kmara copied Otpor and Pora copied Kmara. As Georgian opposition leader Ivane Merabishvili recounts, "all the demonstrators knew the tactics of the revolution in Belgrade by heart. Everyone knew what to do. This was a copy of that revolution, only louder." Until recently, courageous young Arab activists had nothing to copy. That changed, finally, on January 14, 2011, the day that Tunisians toppled President Zine El-Abidine Ben Ali.

The model, boiled down to its essence, is devastatingly simple: bring enough people into the streets and overwhelm the regime with sheer numbers. "No state," observes sociologist Charles Kurzman, "can repress all of the people all of the time." Once protesters reach a critical mass, the regime finds itself in a precarious situation. The decision to shoot may temporarily push back protesters, but it is a risky course. The use of lethal force can provide the spark for an embattled opposition, as on Iran's 'Black Friday,' when around a hundred Iranians were killed on the way to their revolution.

Such violence threatens to strip regimes of their last shreds of legitimacy. It also creates sympathy for opposition groups and their cause, spurring financial, moral, and political support from the international community. More importantly, the use of live ammunition on unarmed citizens can often provoke divisions within the regime coalition.

Inevitably, some in the security forces or the military will refuse to obey orders. In the case of Tunisia, the army was simply not willing to oversee a bloodbath to protect President Ben Ali. In the uprising against Libyan leader Muammar Gadhafi that gained momentum in February, the Libyan regime shot down hundreds of peaceful protesters. The move generated an immediate backlash against Gadhafi by the U.S. and other Western powers, which in recent years had reestablished relations with his regime. As the Filipino opposition figure Francisco Nemenzo once wrote, "It is one thing to shoot peasants in some God-forsaken village and another to massacre middle class dissenters while the whole world is watching."

International outrage, then, is an essential ingredient. Before the Tunisian revolution, however, it had been almost entirely missing in the peculiar context of the Arab world. With few exceptions, the most popular movements in the Arab world have been led by Islamists, and for Western powers this made them more difficult to support. At the height of international interest in the first 'Arab Spring,' Egypt experienced the largest pro-democracy mobilization it had seen in decades. On March 27, 2005, the Muslim Brotherhood staged its first ever protest calling for constitutional reform, after the ruling party forced through amendments that restricted opposition groups' ability to contest presidential elections. By May, the organization had staged twenty-three demonstrations—an average of one every three days—in fifteen governorates. Some brought out as many as fifteen thousand people. On May 4, the Brotherhood staged a coordinated nationwide protest in ten governorates, with an estimated fifty to seventy thousand protestors. In the course of less than two months, the total participation of Brotherhood members neared one hundred and forty thousand.

Such a show of strength came at a price: nearly four thousand Brotherhood members were arrested. Yet, the international community was largely silent. Paying a high price, the Brotherhood learned its lesson. If that's what happened when the world was watching, what about when it wasn't?

The New Opposition

In Tunisia, the Ben Ali regime couldn't use the Islamist card. Tunisia's Islamists were either in prison, dead, or in exile. By destroying its main opposition, the regime lost the last justification for its existence. Ben Ali couldn't argue that he was better than the alternative, because there was no alternative left.

In Egypt, the Muslim Brotherhood, despite its widespread following, played a significant but relatively limited role in the protests, which it did not endorse until after the success of the first day—January 25—was already apparent. Like Tunisia, Egypt's was a leaderless movement consisting of angry, ordinary Egyptians who came not with ideologies or partisanship but the simple, overarching demand that President Mubarak step down. Predictably, the regime tried to point the finger at the Brotherhood but the reality in Tahrir Square belied such claims.

That these were leaderless revolutions meant that the regimes had no one to demonize, except their own people. If they shot into the crowd, they were not killing the Muslim Brotherhood but their own brothers, sisters, sons, and daughters. And when they did kill—over two hundred in Tunisia and at least three hundred eighty-four in Egypt—allied Western powers (and the international media) could no longer turn away.

While Arabs have long blamed the West, and particularly the United States, for supporting their oppressors, this was perhaps the one case where American support ultimately worked to their favor. The Egyptian military and security forces did not enjoy full freedom of action. The U.S., as Egypt's primary benefactor, was watching closely. The Obama administration may have had a high tolerance for regime repression, but it was unlikely to tolerate massacres against peaceful protesters in broad daylight. This, whether indirectly or directly, exerted pressure on regime officials who had to make difficult choices on whether to use force against protesters. The close relationship between the U.S. and Egyptian militaries also offered another important point of leverage in the crucial final days of the revolution, when the military had to decide whether to turn on Mubarak, one of their own.

Lessons from the Revolution

In Tunisia and then Egypt, Arabs discovered a power they did not know they had. These revolutions, as others before them, told a story of strength and safety in numbers. There was no need to follow a sequence—economic reform first, democracy later—or meet a long list of prerequisites. Arabs, it turns out, did not have to wait for democracy. More importantly, they didn't want to. The hundreds of millions of dollars in civil society aid had been rendered beside the point. America's caution, hedging of bets, and fetish for gradualism—previously the hallmarks of hard-headed realpolitik—proved both foolhardy and naïve. Of course, Americans always said they knew this: freedom and democracy was not the province of one people or culture, but a universal right.

To Al-Qaeda's dismay, real change does not come through violence. But it doesn't necessarily come through NGOs. Arabs kept on waiting for America to change its policy and divest itself of dictatorship. It never did. So they did. In doing so, they are forcing the U.S. to reconsider five decades of a failed, and failing, policy in the Middle East.

It would be a mistake, though, to conclude that international factors are now irrelevant. In the cases of Egypt, Tunisia, and Libya, international pressure, whether from governments or citizens moved by what they saw on television, played a critical role in undermining support for regimes that just months before were thought by many to be invulnerable.

The revolutions are far from complete. Tunisia has faced sporadic violence and a succession of unstable interim cabinets. Despite being the original spark for the region's uprisings, it has, perhaps predictably, become the forgotten revolution. Egypt is still governed by an institution—the military—that was long the backbone of the Mubarak regime. For many Egyptian activists, March 9 was a turning point, bringing back painful memories. That day, soldiers and plainclothes thugs armed with pipes and electric cables stormed Tahrir Square, detained nearly two hundred people, and then took them to be tortured in a makeshift prison at the Egyptian Museum. As their challenges grow, the country's opposition groups have returned to their old fractious ways. Indeed, democratic transitions are notoriously messy and uncertain. Recognizing this, the Arab world's new emerging democracies will need support and assistance from the international community, including the U.S. This can be done through technical assistance and election monitoring. But more high-level involvement may be necessary as well, by putting pressure on the new governments to uphold their commitments and providing financial incentives to meet certain benchmarks on democratization. The question is whether the U.S. and its European allies, with their cash-strapped governments and skeptical publics, are willing to commit billions of dollars to helping democratize a still-troubled region.

A great deal is at stake. America was rightly credited for helping facilitate transitions in many Eastern European and Latin American countries. If the U.S. is seen as helping make another transition possible, this time in Egypt, Tunisia, and elsewhere, it will give Americans much-needed credibility in the region. Successful transitions could herald a reimagined relationship between the U.S. and the Arab world, something that Obama promised in his 2009 Cairo address but failed to deliver on.

To be sure, the United States has a checkered, tragic history in the region. For decades, the U.S. has been on the wrong side of history, supporting and funding Arab autocrats and undermining nascent democratic movements when they threatened American interests. So critics of Western 'meddling' have a point: whenever the U.S. and Europe interfere in the region, they seem to get it wrong. That is precisely why it's so important that, this time, they get it right. But getting it right requires that the U.S. fundamentally reassess its Middle East policy and align itself with Arab populations and their democratic aspirations. This has not happened.

Egypt and Tunisia, despite all their problems, remain the most promising cases. Elsewhere, the situation is considerably more grave, with U.S.-backed autocrats in Yemen and Bahrain having used unprecedented force against their own citizens. Saudi Arabia's military intervention in Bahrain has fanned the flames of regional sectarianism and made an already explosive situation even worse.

Thus far, the Obama administration has been behind the curve in nearly every country, reacting to rather than shaping events. President Obama adopted a slow and deliberate approach, and refused to take a stronger stand with America's

Yemeni and Gulf allies. Even enemies such as the Syrian regime have so far escaped any real pressure. If anything is clear, it is that Arabs have shown that something more than caution and gradualism is called for in historic moments of change. This time, they–not the international community–are leading the way. But they and their countries need the international community to follow. Otherwise, their revolutions may still fail.

---

1 Stephen McInerney, "The President's Budget Request for Fiscal Year 2009: Democracy, Governance, and Human Rights in the Middle East," Project on Middle East Democracy, May 2008.

2 Daniel Brumberg, "Liberalization Versus Democracy: Understanding Arab Political Reform," Carnegie Endowment, May 2003, p. 13

3 Michael McFaul, "Ukraine Imports Democracy: External Influences on the Orange Revolution," *International Security* 32 (Fall 2007): pp. 45–83

4 Steven Levitsky and Lucan A. Way, *Competitive Authoritarianism: Hybrid Regimes after the Cold War* (Cambridge, UK: Cambridge University Press, 2010)

Reflections on Arab Renaissance

A Call for Education Reform

By Ahmed Zewail

I recently read an important study that left me in awe of the knowledge demographics of our planet. In *Educating All Children: A Global Agenda*, Joel Cohen and David Bloom argue that while the aim of achieving primary and secondary schooling for all children is urgent and feasible, more than three hundred million children will not be in school in the year 2015. Empowering future generations with contemporary liberal arts education represents a significant challenge, even for highly developed nations. A year ago, President Barack Obama announced a major expansion of Educate to Innovate, a program to raise, in the coming decade, the level of American students in science, technology, engineering, and mathematics, or STEM, as the disciplines are collectively known. One of the new initiatives of the project is to spend more than $250 million of public and private funds to prepare ten thousand new teachers and retrain more than one hundred thousand others in the fields of math and science. As a presidential advisor, I know that the Obama administration has made all levels of education, an enterprise of nearly a trillion dollar budget, one of its top priorities.

For the Arab world, good education is critical for making our future. The failure of Arab education is one of the underlying causes of the youth discontent we are witnessing throughout the region. The serious cultural, economic, and political consequences have become obvious. The children of Facebook have ignited an intifada to plant democracy in Egypt, Tunisia, Bahrain, Yemen, Libya and other Arab countries. Only when we diagnose the symptoms can we cure the disease, and it is education that is at the core of any recovery—an Arab renaissance. It is imperative and a matter of urgency that education be elevated to a much higher national priority throughout the Middle East. Anyone who examines the progress achieved in Europe, the United States, or in more recently developed nations

▷ Physics class at the German University in Cairo, March 1, 2006. *Gary Knight/VII/Corbis*

in Asia or Latin America, can understand the direct correlation between good education and the development of societies. Indeed, Egypt is a living testimony to the link between the power of knowledge and the impact of its ancient civilization—and that later one established on the shores of the Mediterranean some two thousand years ago, in Alexandria, whose library and museum constituted a beacon of knowledge.

The concept of civilization itself is based upon knowledge. On the banks of the river Nile, the ancient Egyptians introduced new concepts in fields such as architecture, medicine, astronomy, and chemistry that influenced the Pharaonic as well as later civilizations. In my own field, some six thousand years ago, they were the first to ingeniously measure time and create the solar calendar. Recently, French scientists reported yet another astounding achievement, namely that the eye cosmetics used in the time of Nefertiti contained a man-made lead compound that helped treat or prevent eye disease. The modern West continues to explore the progress attained by this ancient civilization.

Arab civilization, a millennium ago, recorded outstanding achievements as well. Last year, I published with Sir John Thomas of the University of Cambridge a book about four-dimensional microscopy imaging. In this book and elsewhere I point out that major contributions to the science of imaging and vision were made by the Muslim thinker Ibn al-Haytham (known in the West as Alhazen) who lived ca. 965–1040 in Iraq and Egypt. He developed concepts in optics, later used by Descartes, Newton, Da Vinci, and our modern photographers, that explain how the retina works to receive an image from reflected light. His experiment, called *al-hugra al-muzlima*, "the dark room," later known as camera obscura, demonstrated how external light passing through a pinhole in a box forms an upside-down image on an interior surface. The making of useful knowledge by Ibn al-Haytham, Ibn Rushd (the polymath philosopher known in the West as Averroës), Ibn Sina (the foremost physician of his time, known as Avicenna), al-Khawarizmi (whose Latinized name, Algoritmi, inspired the terms algorism and algorithm), and other renaissance men, forged centers of enlightenment in capitals such as Baghdad, Cairo, and Cordoba.

Modern Egypt, too, was recognized for a renaissance in educational, cultural, and industrial fields, in part due to the progress made possible by the visionary leadership of Mohammed Ali. He transformed Egypt into a regional industrial and military power through reorganization and reforms in the society and by means of educational and cultural missions from Egypt to Europe. Rifa'a al-Tahtawi and his followers were among the pioneers in bringing about a renaissance in education with the aid of knowledge translated from French into Arabic. In the years to follow, Egypt became a powerhouse in literature, arts, science, and culture. Personalities in all fields emerged and influenced Arab society at large. We still live on the echoes of their contributions, from the writings of Taha Hussein, Naguib Mahfouz, and Ali Moustafa Mosharafa, to the songs and films of Umm Kulthum, Abdel Wahab, and Faten Hamama. In the Middle East, only a century ago, Egypt pioneered democratic governance and established institutions in different sectors of higher education and scientific research (Cairo University), banking (Bank al-Ahly), mass media (Al-Ahram), and industries such as textile and the motion picture. With this advanced status, Egypt attracted and educated future generations of Arabs, including, among many others, the renowned Palestinian Edward W. Said, Michael Atiyah of Lebanon, King Hussein of Jordan, and my own father-in-law Chaker El-Faham of Syria. As recently as the 1960s, after the 1952 revolution, my generation benefited from a fine education system amid a rich cultural life and national dreams of colossal projects, such as the High Dam, space aviation, and nuclear energy.

A Bleak Situation

With these past achievements in mind, and knowing that human resources are still available, one has to ask what happened to education and scientific research in the modern Arab world? Today, the contribution of the Arab world to international scientific research is negligible. In both research investment (R&D spend compared to GDP) and capacity (researcher numbers compared to population), as reflected in research publication output between 2000 and 2009, the predominance of Turkey and Iran is evident; in 2009 Turkey produced twenty-two thousand publications as compared to five thousand in 2000, and Iran produced fifteen thousand papers in 2009, in vast contrast to thirteen hundred in 2000. During the same period Egypt and Saudi Arabia had a flat trajectory at nearly two thousand, according to a very recent global research report by Thomson Reuters. No Arab university regularly ranks among the world's five hundred best institutions, though Alexandria University made it in one ranking in 2010. Ibrahim El-Moallem, vice president of the International Publishers Association, estimates that book sales in the Arab world are 1 percent of the world market (Egypt accounts for 0.4 percent), and that books of basic sciences and arts are only 3 to 5 percent of total sales. Egypt's national income from research and development is minor. The GDP depends on revenues from traffic in the Suez Canal, tourism, and natural resources such as gas and oil, all a "gift of the Nile," as Herodotus called the land of Egypt. By contrast, Israel, with less than a tenth of Egypt's eighty-million population, acquires more than 90 percent of its GDP primarily from industry and services, with technology being the back bone of the economy.

Current conditions do not encourage optimism if we consider government expenditures. On basic education, according to a report by the renowned medical doctor Mohamed Ghoneim, based on United Nations Development Programme data, the

Egyptian government spends annually twenty-four billion Egyptian pounds (less than $5 billion and around 2.4 percent of the national income) which amounts to about $250 per student per year. Israel, to make another comparison, spends at least $1,500 per student per year. At university level, the Egyptian government spends less than $500 per year on each of its 2.2 million students. In contrast, Egyptians are paying $15,000 and $10,000, respectively, for private education at the American University in Cairo or the Nile University, for example. Such is the bleak situation in public education that causes Egyptian families to pay between ten and fifteen billion Egyptian pounds per year for private tutoring in the hopes of giving their children a greater chance to learn and succeed.

The infrastructure of most of the Egyptian schools is far behind a country like Finland or South Korea. The number of students in public-school classes reaches sixty and more, making it impossible for a teacher to interact well with pupils. University lecture halls are packed with hundreds of students. Teaching also relies heavily on indoctrination, failing to take advantage of pedagogical methodologies that have advanced throughout the modern world. Many of the topics in the curriculum are not suitable, especially when we consider that these students have to compete in the information and space age.

In Egypt, teachers have an unfavorable financial position and a lower-than-ever social status. Even with a recent salary increase, many find themselves forced to offer private lessons on the side as a way of supplementing their incomes. What is needed are teachers, or *mu'allims*, who can cognitively attract students to new ideas and knowledge, not simply tutors who prepare them for rote memorization and passing exams.

Society and Media

Conditions in Arab society at large have not been very conducive to advancement in education. More than 35 percent of the Arab population is under the age of fifteen. This represents a potential boom in human resources, yet it is not effectively utilized. The unemployment rate in the region ranges from 10 to 20 percent. Egyptian families face a greater burden in raising children today compared to fifty years ago. In an estimated 30 percent of the families, women are the breadwinners due to issues like divorce.

The Arab media are not equipped to perform their responsibility to illuminate educational and scientific matters, despite the increasing number of newspapers, magazines, and over five hundred television satellite channels (most of them concerned with music video clips and soap operas). A few years ago I happened to arrive in Egypt right after the landing of the NASA rover, Opportunity, on Mars. The world seemed transfixed by this remarkable event, but in Egypt I could only find a small story about it in one of the newspapers. It is generally acknowledged that the search for truth and in-depth analysis are uncommon features in the programming of the influential broadcast media, which consume about one-third of the day in the life of the average Egyptian. In a recent TV program watched by millions, the anchorman said we must find out "who changed the weather" (*min illi ghayyar al-gaww*) to make it so bad, adding in all seriousness "We must deal immediately with the culprit or the country involved!"

The culture is under pressure. One of my concerns is that we are creating subcultures within the Arab culture. In private schools, which are now becoming a major force in Arab education, the language used and culture practiced are often those of other nations. Of course it is proper to teach foreign languages, yet without proper education in the Arabic language and traditions, the country risks class/language fragmentation in society. I also see blind imitation as another threat to the culture of the Arab world. If MTV in America (which incidentally does not reflect the rich American culture) airs certain programming, it does not mean that Arab society is not modern unless its channels offer the same thing. The quest for modernization must respect cultural identity.

In the realm of religious values, the vital role of true religion has been replaced by ideological stubbornness and, I may say, ideological terrorism by some. I believe that the use of politics in religion and religion in politics is creating confusion and conflict in society. The spread of rulings or pronouncements from non-qualified proselytizers has diverted society's energy into superficial issues and led to calcification of the mind. And evasion of the rule of law has had many consequences. The most threatening of all is 'societal fragmentation,' which has led to cracks in national unity through bigotry and violence, as we saw in Nag Hammadi and Alexandria in Egypt. Superficial media rhetoric does not solve problems and people must use reason to reach their goals for national coherence and civil society governance. One essential change is good education.

A Paradigm Shift

It is clear that the education system is in need of major reform. In any nation, schooling can generally be categorized into primary and secondary education, higher education, and research and development, normally involving Master's and Ph.D. degree studies.

Primary Education

Basic education is a human right, especially in the knowledge society of today. It must be a priority for governments to embark on a major national project to eliminate illiteracy. I find it hard to believe or understand, in an age seeking ever greater scientific knowledge, that from 25 to 50 percent of the Arab population of some three hundred and fifty million remains illiterate. How can this population at large deal with the modern world of services through the internet, or be effective in the knowledge-based work force? How can illiterate parents prepare the children of tomorrow?

Arabs need to dramatically increase spending on education. In most of the Arab countries, the current low percentage of national wealth spent on education will never improve the schools, curricula, and teachers to produce the kinds of students that are equipped to handle national and international demands. More resources are needed, and they should have priority over less essential projects like mega-resorts for luxury living. The allocation of new resources must be directed with care to enhance quality over quantity.

The status of teachers must change through a merit-based system of evaluation and appreciation. That should eliminate the present parallel education system of private tutors, upon whom Egyptian middle-class families spend a disproportionate amount of their income to enhance an education that is supposedly free. The involvement of the private sector should take on a new structure, one that creates a partnership between schools and families and involves them in the education process; no single person, not even a minister, knows the answers to questions pertinent to the most effective mechanisms in education.

Higher Education

Higher education with hundreds of thousands of university students and low-level resources has proved to be ineffective. It is time to restructure the current organization, which was effective half a century ago, and to create a modern multi-tier system of public and private higher education. For public education, it would be reasonable to establish three or four tiers of universities with the layers being defined according to students' ability and social situation. On the other hand, private universities should not be for business; in fact, they should represent the pinnacle of education, research, and development as nonprofit organizations.

In California, for example, the state supports the University of California and California State University systems, community colleges, and others such as adult education schools. Each of them has its own goals and mission; the aim of educating a student going to Berkeley is different from that at Cal State, Los Angeles, or Pasadena City College. In the end, the students will get educations that serve them and the society. But depending on ability, status, and presence on campus (full/part time), the student and the state are in a position to tailor needs and effectiveness. Parents who can afford their children's university fees should be required to make financial contributions, just as they do when their children are enrolled in private universities at home or abroad, but those students who do not have the means should acquire appropriate education either through merit-based scholarships or from a loan-granting banking system.

Also in California, again by way of example, there exist some of the best private universities in the world, including Caltech and Stanford. Besides the excellent education they offer, and the enabling of the thinkers behind Intel, Google, and other mega-companies, they represent powerhouses for global research and development. Both Caltech and Stanford are nonprofit private universities. Their support comes from endowment, philanthropy, and relatively high tuition. For research, both public and private institutions receive funding mostly from federal government agencies and the private sector. The National Science Foundation is a key source of funding, and Arab countries should establish similar entities for funding independent and creative research. I also suggest defense ministries develop funding programs, as a percentage of their total budget, for national support of R&D even if the research is only remotely related to the defense issues of today.

In the region, Israel and Turkey have succeeded in establishing advanced private institutions. In Turkey, Bilkent University is a leading research institution, whose endowment is sustained by income from major international projects such as the construction of world-class airports (for example in Cairo and Doha) and the supply of high-tech products to various industries. Such a concept was proposed as a national project in Egypt more than ten years ago; more details can be found in my book, *'Asr al-'ilm*. With independent institutions, Israel has become a high-tech superpower over the past two decades. Scaling to its population, it leads the world in number of start-ups and size of venture-capital industry. The Israeli government has now identified new frontiers of focus, including areas of potential growth, in alternative energy, water management, agricultural innovations, and of course in the military industry.

Teaching methodology in higher education is in need of revamping. Understanding of and respect for facts is essential for the scientific method, which is not only important for education itself but also for integrating rational thinking into the fabric of the culture.

In countries with overpopulated universities, students are not provided with "hands on" opportunities for involvement in learning. When I was a student at Alexandria University, I was in a special class of seven students and had direct access to microscopes, experiments, and the like. Today, with the large number of students involved, carefully instituted and interactive teaching methods can enable students to perform experiments through virtual reality technology. Such methods, which I have observed in Turkey and Malaysia, represent a totally different and better way for cognitive involvement than teaching students science largely through memorization. Faculty must be equipped with the latest techniques, through retraining and periodic updating, and perhaps through sabbatical leave. Such faculty are to be evaluated and academically and financially rewarded according to performance.

To increase the level of skill nationwide, technical and vocational education must be enhanced and respected. This type of education empowers the society with know-how and improves the infrastructure. It is also time to stop admitting more students than universities have the capacity to teach, and to end the exaggeration of scores in obtaining degrees. In the 1960s, it was a great achievement for me to score over 90 percent in my bachelor's degree. Now we hear of 110 percent scores! Scientifically, 100 percent is the maximum meaningful score. I can understand so-called bonuses, but these should not be confused with actual grades.

Finally, the reform of higher education should begin with the restoring of the prestige of the university and faculty and by raising the admissions standards. I recall how emotional I felt on my arrival at the campus of the Faculty of Science, because of the high standing, the *hayba*, the university and faculty had in our society at that time. The campus should be the home of knowledge and culture, not a space for political and religious conflicts. It need not be policed for security. In all universities I am familiar with, students can have intellectual discourses on all subjects and organize all kinds of events under the supervision of their mentors and subject to university by-laws, and, if extra precautions are needed, these take the form of campus security staff, not a police force.

Research and Development Centers

The third and final level of the education pyramid is scientific research. First, we should clarify a few misconceptions. No nation can establish a viable R&D program without commitment from its government in the form of long-term investment. In fact, without such backing I cannot see why the public in general and the private sector in particular should contribute to funding R&D. Second, developing nations can achieve progress on the international level in a relatively short time, contrary to the belief that such progress requires one or two generations. The proof came recently from a number of countries including China, India, South Korea, Malaysia, and now Turkey and Iran. Third, R&D is not a luxury, as some believe, reserved for rich or developed countries. This too is proved false, since developing, and in many cases poor, countries have crossed the chasm that divides them from developed nations by investing *more* generously in R&D. Fourth, there is a fundamental role for basic research in development, and this cannot be strong without a science base that integrates expertise in STEM.

Curiosity-driven basic research requires that creative scientists work in an environment that encourages interactions between researchers and collaborations across different fields. But such attributes cannot and should not be orchestrated by structured and weighty management, as creative minds and bureaucracies are incompatible. Large buildings alone will not produce much without the right people. To distract faculty members with excessive regulations, research for-promotion incentives, or to involve them as political tools, is the beginning of the end. Without resources little can be achieved, no matter how creative the mind. Countries and institutions that provide the proper infrastructure and the funding for new ideas will be the home of new discoveries and the source of innovations.

The quest for new knowledge drives innovation, and without centers of excellence, young students and scientists will not be attracted to the profession of R&D. My own attraction to science was enhanced by the sheer joy of discovery, which began in Egypt with a school-age curiosity about why wood burns. When I look back and ask why Caltech, or the California Institute of Technology, where I have spent the last thirty years of my career, has garnered thirty-five Nobel prizes, it is because Caltech as an institution believes in such values. Its unique culture makes scholars enjoy the quest for the unknown, free from bureaucratic regulations and political hierarchy.

It is time for Egypt and other Arab countries to have such a vision and for governments to be determined to allocate substantial resources to establish R&D centers of excellence. These centers should be rising with at least equal priority to the media megacities recently brought into existence in several Arab capitals. As importantly, the centers must be granted independence in order to formulate their own academic and administrative structures. Among other things, establishing a merit system for scholars and elevating the prestige of the chair professor are important essentials. For young researchers, the government should increase the number of scientific missions it sends abroad. In turn, the research environment should be attractive to the scholars when they return to their homeland with the benefits of the knowledge they have acquired. Their missions abroad are a waste of money if they are forced to struggle with bureaucratic obstacles back home.

The Knowledge Chasm

In the Arab world, we face the daunting challenge of reducing the knowledge gap with the rest of the world in many fields of endeavor. When I was a graduate student, America, after the launch of the Russian sputnik, had a vision to conquer outer space, and in 1969 Neil Armstrong walked on the moon. Today, America is sending space cars and possibly an astronaut to Mars. Scientists are searching for life on other planets with the potential of finding new resources or, in the case of some governments, with the desire to control the Earth from outer space.

In the field of medicine, discoveries are made at the level of genes and cells, opening up new avenues for drug design and cures for disease. Today, scientists can take adult cells from skin and convert them into stem cells that can be used to develop new tissues for the heart, eyes, and other parts of our bodies. Such discoveries were unimaginable twenty years ago.

In the microscopic world of nanotechnology, for the first time in human history, man can visualize objects in four dimensions, functioning on a time scale of a millionth of a billionth of a second, and in their 3-D space with a better than one-billionth-of-a-meter precision. This methodology, which my group and I developed recently at Caltech, has the potential of uncovering new phenomena in materials science and in biological/medical sciences.

These are just a few examples that demonstrate the chasm between the haves and the have-nots of knowledge. It would be naïve to think that the quest for useful knowledge is a luxury for society. Exploring for its own sake enables humans to discover the "unknown unknowns," and not simply to polish our knowledge of the "known unknowns."

Epilogue

Civilizations rise through the power of knowledge. They fall when such power fades. Arab and Muslim civilizations reached their zenith when their leaders believed in the value of making new knowledge and in ensuring human rights and liberty of mind, the necessary tools for progress. Preserving knowledge is easy. Transferring knowledge is also easy. But making new knowledge is neither easy nor profitable—in the short term. It has, however, proved to be hugely profitable in the long run. Think of the impact of only two curiosity-driven discoveries, the laser and the transistor, which have now transformed world markets and human services. And there is more: knowledge is a force that enriches the culture of any society with reason and basic truth and enlightens people against bigotry and radicalism.

In the modern era, the Arab people have not been makers of useful knowledge, and they are facing major challenges. Some of these are crippling their influence and participation in the world market and others are threatening the foundation of their own culture. At the core of the problem is the challenge of a deteriorating education system. Without education there is no progress and progress does not lie in the ability to consume and acquire goods from abroad. Arabs are in need of a renaissance that is built on a modern education and a science base with its triad of basic research, technology transfer, and societal involvement.

The impossible is possible. I certainly have confidence that Egypt can succeed despite all the complexities and problems in education and scientific research, and in governance. Turkey and Iran are emerging as a real force in the Middle East, and without Egypt's force the Arabs will not be in the sphere of influence. Some Arab and Muslim countries, including Qatar, Turkey, and Malaysia, have already made progress in the field of education, transcending the stereotypes currently associated with Muslim culture and religion. But no country can cut corners to development. Important changes and progress in the Arab world will only occur if there is a political vision and will from the highest levels of the state. In the past, and we in the Arab world have all experienced this, it was possible to enclose a whole country. Today, that is impossible. The poor and the rich alike have small satellite dishes on their roofs, which show them how things are around the world. The sky and the whole world are open to our children. The political upheaval in the Arab world is telling of the need for a speedy change.

As we work toward a better future, there should be no conflict between science and religion. Education, which etymologically derives from the Latin "to bring out" potential, is any act or experience that has a formative effect on the mind, character, or physical ability of an individual. Education eradicates ideological stubbornness. In Arabic the word *ta'lim* captures its essence; it is from *'ilm*, or knowledge. Education is the process by which society deliberately transmits its accumulated knowledge, skills, and values from one generation to another. It is therefore in the fabric of civilization. We should make use of the minds humans are uniquely blessed with, and accept faith and reason as the bases for human life. Egypt utilized both in building its ancient civilization. It must do so again.

Taha Hussein, one of our great writers, said decades ago, "*al-'ilm ka-l-maa wa-l-hawa'.*" ("Education is a necessity, like the water we drink and the air we breathe.") Without *'ilm*, there is no life. Arabs have an opportunity to regain their place in history. The reasons for backwardness are several. Colonization and occupation have certainly been part of the problem. The self interest of superpowers, and even uninformed prejudices against cultures or ethnic groups, have always been in the fabric of politics. But we cannot live in the past or in the present with conspiracy theories. We must first solve our in-house problems in order to light the future. With "Liberty, Knowledge, and Faith" (the motto of the Ahmed Zewail Foundation for Knowledge and Development in Cairo), I believe that Arab renaissance will launch the dawning of a new age. The choice is ours: either to become three hundred and fifty million people of the cave, *ahl al-kahf*, or three hundred and fifty million people of the cosmos, *ahl al-kawn*.

This article is based on addresses given by the author at the Dubai Press Club and at the Cairo Opera House in 2010.

THE ISRAELI-PALESTINIAN CONFLICT NOW

How President Obama can get peacemaking back on track

By William B. Quandt

The upheaval that shook the Arab world in early 2011 should lead to a fundamental recalibration of American policies in the Middle East. As this debate gets underway, many, perhaps most, will conclude that this is no time for pushing hard for Arab-Israeli peace. They will argue that it is time to let the dust from the Arab revolution settle, to shore up other fragile regimes, and to hope for the best. Certainly the official view from Israel will reinforce such a wait and see attitude. But such a posture, at a time like this, will have the effect of making the United States look marginal to the central developments of the region.

While it is true that U.S. influence has waned in recent years–and that need not be such a bad thing–on the issue of Arab-Israeli peace the U.S. still has a major interest and a major responsibility. So, the Obama administration should take a hard look, screw up its courage, and try for a serious multi-pronged effort to get Arab-Israeli peacemaking onto a promising track. If successful–and the odds are admittedly not good–this would mean that the U.S. was aligning itself with both democracy and peace in a vital part of the world. That would go a long way toward securing American interests. But, is it doable?

The president still has time to make mid-course corrections and start to move in a more promising direction. But time is short and he will have to recognize some of the serious errors he has made if he is to get things right. To have a chance of success, Obama must mobilize a major internationally supported initiative to lay out the broad guidelines, in the form of quite specific principles, for the resolution of both the Israeli–Palestinian conflict and the Israeli–Syrian one as well.

What went wrong? After all, Obama as a presidential candidate in 2008 seemed to be genuinely committed to trying a new approach to peacemaking. And he seemed

◁ President Barack Obama and Israeli Prime Minister Benjamin Netanyahu at the White House, May 18, 2009. *Lawrence Jackson/White House/CNP/Corbis*

to understand that Arab–Israeli peace would make a big dent in the intense anti-Americanism that could be found in much of the Arab and Islamic worlds.

Obama got off to a good start in January 2009. He supported the idea of engagement with adversaries, mentioning Iran and Syria by name, and privileging diplomacy over military force. He appointed a respected and experienced former senator, George Mitchell, to oversee the day-to-day conduct of his Arab–Israeli policy. As the national security advisor he named General James Jones, a man with considerable experience with the Palestine issue. In a number of public statements, Obama made it clear that he wanted to move forcefully toward Arab–Israeli peace and he took a particularly firm stand on an issue of great importance to the Palestinians, namely the need for Israel to stop building settlements in occupied territory. Obama's new approach was aptly expressed in his June 4, 2009 speech at Cairo University, in which he said: "I have come here to seek a new beginning between the United States and Muslims around the world, one based upon mutual interest and mutual respect."

While all of these steps raised hopes in some quarters that American policy was moving into a new and active phase, there were also some warning signs that events might force the new president to trim his ambitions. First there was the obvious fact that the global economic crisis, which significantly worsened in the months before his election, was bound to occupy much of his time and energy. In addition to pushing a stimulus package and bank bailouts to address the economic crisis, his domestic political agenda included passing legislation on health care. These proved also to be difficult and divisive tasks, quickly drawing down on the president's political capital.

In the Middle East, two elections also made it more difficult for the president to proceed with his initial strategy. First, in Israel, elections resulted in the return of hard-line Likud leader, Benjamin Netanyahu, to the prime minister's office. He had served as prime minister in the period 1996–1999 and had strenuously resisted U.S. efforts to move forward on Israeli–Palestinian peace talks. To say the least, his reputation in Washington was that of a stubborn and unimaginative leader who was unwilling to take risks for peace.

The other election that damaged the chances for Obama to pursue his plans to engage constructively with adversaries took place in Iran in June 2009 and was widely viewed in the West as a deeply flawed affair that cheated the reformist movement of a possible victory. Instead of dealing with Iranian moderates, Obama would have to deal with a reinstated President Mahmoud Ahmadinejad and Supreme Leader Ayatollah Ali Khamenei. Many Americans were highly skeptical about the wisdom of trying to pursue a policy of engagement with this Iranian regime, especially as it continued to follow a policy of producing nuclear energy that led many to believe Iran was on its way to becoming a nuclear weapons state in violation of its commitments under the Non-Proliferation Treaty.

The Netanyahu Problem

Obama and Netanyahu did not get off to a very good start. With some effort, Obama did help persuade Netanyahu to express guarded support for the so-called 'two-state solution' to the Israeli–Palestinian conflict, but he had a much harder time persuading the Israeli prime minister to stop building settlements in the West Bank and east Jerusalem. This latter point became a test of wills between the two leaders, and finally in late 2009 Netanyahu gave a partial concession—a moratorium on new settlement construction in the West Bank (but not east Jerusalem) for a period of ten months. By the time this offer was made, Obama and his political advisors were showing signs of being worried about the prolonged strain in U.S.–Israeli relations. Many seemed to feel that it was time for the president to mend fences and to accept what Netanyahu had offered as a positive first step. Secretary of State Hillary Clinton, long attuned to the domestic politics surrounding the management of the relationship with Israel from her time as senator from New York state, was quick to label Netanyahu's offer of a ten-month moratorium as "unprecedented"—which was not true—and to turn to the Palestinians with demands that they agree to enter negotiations.

During the first part of 2010, there was very little real movement in Arab–Israeli peace diplomacy. Mitchell travelled diligently to the region, but his style was so low-key that whatever gains he made were barely noticed. In mid year, Obama and Netanyahu met in Washington for a carefully staged reconciliation meeting. With Congressional elections on the horizon, Obama presumably did not want to burden Democratic candidates with the charge that the Obama administration was excessively tough in its dealings with Israel. Exactly what happened during the meeting between the two leaders is not clear. It seems that Netanyahu made a strong case for U.S. support in confronting Iran; and in return for U.S. assurances on this score, he agreed to enter "direct negotiations without preconditions" with the Palestinians.

White House Middle East advisors began to talk about a "new Netanyahu," a strong leader who would be prepared to make concessions for peace. The "old Netanyahu," a man whose ideological roots are found deep in the revisionist Zionist tradition which sees all of Palestine as rightfully belonging to Israel, had strongly opposed previous peace agreements that his predecessors had negotiated, and had been a very reluctant participant in any talks with the Palestine Liberation Organizaton during his previous tenure as prime minister from 1996 to 1999. Whether this more optimistic view of Netanyahu was based on some serious understandings with him or was more in the nature of wishful thinking could not be determined, but it did mean that U.S. efforts turned to convincing the Palestinians to enter into direct negotiations.

By this time, efforts to engage with Syria had just about dropped off the radar screen. Sound strategy suggests that the U.S. should have done much more to open serious negotiations on the Syrian front—and here negotiation is the right paradigm–and there is a substantial record to build upon. If Syria were also on track to achieving a peace agreement with Israel—the terms of which are much easier to define than they are on the Palestinian front—then Syria would have every incentive to use its influence in support of the peace process. But it was only the Palestinian–Israeli front that received sustained attention, at least in public. As the expiration of the Israeli semi-moratorium on settlement building in the West Bank approached, the American side pressed hard to get negotiations started between Netanyahu and Palestinian President Mahmoud Abbas. Several meetings did take place, but there was no meeting of minds, and when the settlement moratorium expired the Palestinians suspended their participation in the negotiations. By late 2010, the 'peace process' seemed to have reached a stalemate. In fact, it had never gained much momentum at all.

Avoidable Errors

Several things seemed to be wrong with Obama's strategy. First, whatever the wisdom of deciding to make a freeze on settlements his top priority, Obama should have realized that Netanyahu would resist, and that much would depend on who was seen to win this initial test of wills. If Obama were seen to back down on this first issue of contestation, that would damage his reputation for being a strong leader. And back down he did.

Second, Obama did not seem to fully appreciate the importance of having a strong alter ego to serve as his primary diplomat on Arab–Israeli affairs. All prior U.S. successes in Arab–Israeli diplomacy had involved a strong president working closely with an empowered secretary of state, both backed by an experienced team of advisors. This was the model that worked for Nixon–Kissinger, Carter–Vance, and Bush I–Baker. But Obama chose to work with George Mitchell, a low-key technocrat—a man of undoubted ability, but not someone known to be especially close to the president. Hillary Clinton, who might have also played a significant role, seemed stand-offish toward Arab–Israeli issues, at least during her first year as secretary of state.

Recent presidents have allowed a certain amount of chaos to reign among their Arab–Israeli policy group. This was definitely the case for Bill Clinton and Bush II, and it also has been true of Obama. While Mitchell was supposed to be his primary advisor, others were also in the game, often sending rather different signals. There was his first chief of staff, Rahm Emanuel, with close personal ties to Israel; there was his outspoken vice president, Joe Biden, a former chairman of the Senate Foreign Relations Committee; there was his national security advisor, James Jones; and, on at least one occasion, there was General David Petraeus, then head of the U.S. Central Command, on the importance of Arab–Israeli peace to the U.S.'s strategic interests in the Middle East.

And then there was Dennis. In Middle East circles, if you mention the name Dennis it is immediately clear that you are referring to Dennis Ross. No one has logged more hours working on Arab–Israeli issues—starting back in the Reagan administration and then throughout all of Bush I and Clinton. Ross had made an appearance during the campaign as an advisor to Obama on Middle East affairs, but in the initial round of appointments he had been given responsibility at the State Department for a vaguely defined "central region" of the Middle East that seemed to mean Iran and the Gulf region. In any event, with his strongly pro-Israel views, and his reputation for endlessly promoting the "process" part of the peace process, he was not widely seen as the right person to help steer Obama in the new direction that the president seemed to be pursuing. One of his former colleagues described him as a "down in the weeds kind of guy," good for managing the day-to-day diplomacy, but not for charting a new course.

But as U.S.–Israeli relations deteriorated, Ross was called upon to help patch things up with Netanyahu. And by late 2010 he was back in an undefined role at the White House with responsibility for some aspects of Arab–Israeli diplomacy. In short, apart from the president himself, who would have the final word, it was not clear which of his many advisors was key to his plans for getting Arabs and Israelis to make peace.

A third misstep by Obama was to define the Israeli–Palestinian conflict in terms of a dispute that could best be resolved by direct negotiations between the parties. Previous administrations—Clinton and Bush II in particular—had been in the habit of saying that "we cannot want peace more than the parties to the conflict," and that the U.S. would never impose a solution. The U.S. would facilitate, urge, nudge, and persuade, but that was about it. Only in his last month in office did Clinton finally put forward specific proposals. And Bush II, even when he learned that Israelis and Palestinians had made surprising progress in secret talks late in his second term, was unwilling to step in to help clinch the deal.

Obama seemed torn between two paradigms. One saw the Arab–Israeli conflict in strategic terms—its continuation had adverse consequences for U.S. national interests, it weakened moderate forces in the region, gave voice to radicals who whipped up anti-American sentiment, and ultimately made it harder to deal with emerging challenges from countries like Iran or issues like *jihadi* extremism. Obama himself had expressed this view as candidate in 2008 and again in 2009 after his election. From this standpoint, the U.S. could and should place a high priority on solving the conflict, and to do so should use tough-minded diplomacy, including pressures and inducements, to get the parties to move toward compromises. This could be done in cooperation with other powers, the United Nations and regional players, but U.S. power had to be on display for it to work.

There was some reason to believe at the outset of the Obama administration that the president was setting the stage for this type of forceful American-led diplomacy. But somewhere in his second year, Obama seemed to buy into a different paradigm. Like his predecessors, he said frankly that the U.S. could not want Arab–Israeli peace more than the parties themselves. Obama's ambivalence was perfectly captured on April 13, 2010, when he stated that Arab–Israeli peace was a "vital national security interest of the United States," and then also said: "And the truth is, in some of these conflicts the United States can't impose solutions unless the participants in these conflicts are willing to break out of old patterns of antagonism. I think it was former Secretary of State Jim Baker [sic] who said, in the context of Middle East peace, we can't want it more than they do." While this latter point sounds reasonable on the surface, it is in fact a vapid shibboleth. Taken literally, it means that if one party is reticent, that party will set the pace for diplomacy.

But the Arab–Israeli conflict has never been about which party wants peace most. Each community is internally divided over these issues, which are, after all, existential, and many individuals are divided in their own beliefs. They want peace, but they fear the price that they may have to pay to get it. They often seem to want peace in the abstract, but only on their own terms or not at all. This is not the frame for successful face-to-face negotiations. Instead, it suggests the need for a powerful third-party mediator to help structure the negotiations and shift the calculus of gains and losses.

Even with two strong leaders such as Menachem Begin and Anwar Sadat, both of whom doubtless wanted peace on certain terms, it would have been counterproductive for the U. S. to sit back until the two parties had narrowed their differences to the point where the U. S. could step in and help them cross the finish line with a few gentle nudges and reassurances. Had Carter and Vance accepted this model, there would have been no Camp David Summit and no Egyptian–Israeli peace (at least not in 1979).

Perhaps Obama began to focus on getting the parties into direct negotiations as part of a strategy of building American domestic support for a more forceful American role further down the road. But by fall 2010, it sounded very much as if direct negotiations were an end in and of themselves. Many analysts who have studied the Israeli–Palestinian conflict carefully are dubious about the possibility of resolving the conflict through direct negotiations alone. Such a model assumes a degree of parity that does not exist. Israel is in a far stronger position, while the Palestinians are weak, divided, and occupied. The big "concession" made by the Palestinian leadership has been to give up their claim to some 78 percent of historic Palestine and to agree to build their state in the remaining 22 percent. Having come to this point, most Palestinians do not feel there is much more room for concessions on their side. And they continue to insist that their capital must be in east Jerusalem and that some satisfaction must be given, if largely symbolic, to the Palestinian refugees who lost their homes in the 1948 war.

Just as the matter of recovering all of Sinai was never an issue for negotiations in the mind of Anwar Sadat, so also the Palestinians consider these points as fundamental to the question of whether or not a peace agreement is at all possible. Any significant deviation from them will mean peace is an illusion. Where they are prepared to show more flexibility is in the timeline for implementing an agreement; the precise delineation of boundaries, provided that land swaps result in fair compensation for any parts of the west bank that Israel keeps; and on security issues, where the Palestinians are prepared to accept that their future state will never be heavily militarized.

Not surprisingly, Israel sees things very differently. For over forty years, Israel has been in control of east Jerusalem and the West Bank. It sees any relinquishment of these territories as a concession, and no Israeli politician to date has ever publicly accepted the principle of withdrawing to the 1967 lines, including in east Jerusalem. Indeed, many Israeli politicians, including most of the current government, believe in expanding Jewish settlement on the West Bank—a policy interpreted by the Palestinians as intended ultimately to squeeze them out of their homeland. Even the most moderate Israeli leader imagines that some of the West Bank and east Jerusalem will remain under Israeli control indefinitely. And no Israeli leader has said much in public about how Palestinian refugee claims could be addressed. There is very little reason to believe that the parties, given the power imbalance, could bridge the gaps in their positions through direct negotiations. And yet such negotiations have been, as during previous administrations, the centerpiece of American diplomacy.

A fourth mistake, if reports from fall 2010 are true, was that Obama apparently offered some very big inducements to Netanyahu in order to get a mere three-month extension of the settlement moratorium. And even then, Netanyahu refused to comply. This was a sign of Obama's weakness. By prematurely putting some very big chips on the table for very minor purposes, he insured that the price for much bigger moves would soar. This was simply bad bargaining technique. Fortunately, the president seemed to realize his error and was unwilling to put the offer in writing. It was then dropped altogether, along with the demand that Israel cease settlement activity. This left American policy in early 2011 as consisting primarily of the effort to get the parties back to the negotiating table. But this cannot be the sum total of a strategy meant to succeed, especially in the aftermath of the upheaval in Egypt and its regional spillover.

While Obama has little to show for his first two years of Arab–Israeli diplomacy, it is not axiomatic that he cannot make mid-course corrections and start to move in a more promising direction. Surely the popular uprisings in the Middle East have raised understandable questions about whether this is possible right now, yet those upheavals make it all the more important that the U.S. aligns itself with both democracy and peace in a vital part of the world.

Plans for the Third Year

Some have argued that the significant Republican gains in the mid-term elections in November 2010 will make it harder for Obama to govern. On the domestic front this is doubtless so. But Congress is less a factor in setting the broad lines of foreign policy, although there will certainly be some very strong and uncritical pro-Israeli voices elevated to senior positions in Congress. Still, most of what Obama needs to do to improve the odds of success in the Arab–Israeli arena does not depend primarily on Congress.

The President needs to take the following steps:

1. He would need to start making the case immediately that Arab–Israeli peace is in the national interests of the United States. The American public needs to hear a convincing rationale for devoting time and resources to the seemingly hopeless task of breaking the Arab–Israeli impasse.

2. He needs to decide who is going to be his principal spokesman on Arab–Israeli issues. For better or worse, in the current line up of policy advisors, Hillary Clinton is the only person who has the clout to play this role. Mitchell, while genuinely liked and admired, is not viewed as having much real clout by the parties to the dispute.

3. This way of thinking may not be part of the mainstream Washington consensus, but it is frequently expressed behind closed doors, even in the capital. It leads to the conclusion that if there is to be peace, there may be only one last chance and one last policy option: Obama must develop a new American initiative that proposes the outlines of an Israeli–Palestinian accord, as well as a comprehensive Arab–Israeli peace agreement, and mobilize international support behind it. Arab countries moving towards democracy will seek greater purposefulness and fairness in the U.S. diplomatic role in their region, and Obama's failure to anticipate and understand their reasonable expectations will dangerously erode American credibility further at this critical juncture.

The building blocks are all there—the Clinton parameters of December 2000, the outline of an agreement discussed by the then Prime Minister Ehud Olmert and Abbas in fall 2008, the terms of an Israeli–Syrian agreement discussed in detail during 1998–2000. In short, the U.S., with support from others in the international community, would state its support for an agreement that would establish a Palestinian state on the territories of the West Bank and Gaza, with east Jerusalem as its capital. The borders of the state would be based on the 1967 lines, with small agreed adjustments and equitable land swaps. The Palestinian state would recognize Israel and would agree to far-reaching security arrangements, including perhaps international peacekeeping forces at key locations. The hard tradeoff for the Palestinians would be that in exchange for recognition of their state, they would forego the literal "right of return" of refugees to Israel proper, accepting instead some token repatriation and generous compensation for the rest. On the Syrian front, Israel would be expected to withdraw to the June 4, 1967 line, but the Golan would be demilitarized, agreements on water would be worked out, and Syria would be expected to use its influence to help promote a comprehensive Arab–Israeli peace. With these principles clearly spelled out, Arab states would be asked to endorse them and to promise to recognize Israel and establish relations with it as peace with the Palestinians and Syrians goes into effect.

Now, this type of initiative will of course be controversial, particularly among partisans of Israel, who have long maintained that the U. S. should not try to impose its views on the parties. But these points do not really go much beyond what previous American administrations have supported. One could imagine that a fairly impressive bipartisan array of former U.S. officials would support the main outlines of this approach, as would European allies, the so-called Quartet partners (European Union, Russia, and the UN) and the Arab League. One would expect many Palestinians to be generally receptive, although Hamas and other factions will be opposed or skeptical. One should not minimize the difficulty of getting Palestinians to accept the watered-down principle on refugee rights.

The Netanyahu government, and perhaps others in Israel as well, would react negatively at the outset and would try to mobilize opposition to this approach. This is where the test for Obama would begin. Could he convince significant numbers of Israelis that this outline was the best path to a secure, predominantly Jewish democratic state at peace with its neighbors? Could most Israelis be convinced that by accepting this framework, and then negotiating hard on the details and side payments—this is when Obama should be prepared for some major positive inducements—that Israel would be better able to face whatever threat might be posed by Iran?

If Obama is unwilling to see this diplomatic initiative through, he would be better off not launching it. But if he genuinely believes that American national interests are at stake, something along these lines needs to be part of his strategy. We will learn a lot about the president and about American politics by how Obama sets his priorities in the coming months. If there is indeed still a window of opportunity for a comprehensive Arab–Israeli peace, it may not remain open for long. And if Obama does not try to break the impasse, it is unlikely that his eventual successor will do so. The odds of success are not good, based on his efforts of the first two years, but diplomacy is not about playing games with good odds. Occasionally, as now, it would mean tackling a strategically important, difficult issue where both the payoff and risk are high. It is for tackling and successfully resolving such issues that we should bestow the title of statesman. Obama may have won his Nobel peace prize, but if he is to really earn it he should use the undeniable power of the United States to promote the kind of peace agreement outlined here.

NEGOTIATING PEACE IN SUDAN

An American Perspective

By Princeton N. Lyman

In January of this year, nearly four million southern Sudanese went to the polls and voted overwhelmingly for the south to secede from the rest of Sudan. The week-long voting process was peaceful. Observers from around the globe pronounced it free and credible. A new state was about to be born. Yet barely a few months earlier, many feared the referendum would not be allowed to take place or that if it did, rather than a step toward peace, it would be the trigger for renewal of one of Africa's longest civil wars. The danger of renewed war has not entirely ended, but one major step along Sudan's path to peace has been achieved.

Sudan has undergone a long and complicated peace process. Sudan's second civil war between the north and the south ended in 2002. From then to 2011, a nine-year schedule of negotiations and major decisions was laid out. The first agreement was the Machakos protocol in 2002, which provided the basis for a cease-fire and peace negotiations. There followed five more protocols and two appendices negotiated over the next two years, culminating in the signing of the Comprehensive Peace Agreement (CPA) in 2005. Within the CPA was a provision granting the south the right of self-determination, specifically to vote on whether to remain part of Sudan or become independent, on January 9, 2011. The CPA would end in July 2011, when arrangements arising out of the outcome of the referendum were to be completed.

Some have criticized the CPA for being too specific and thus too difficult to implement. Others have criticized its implementation schedule, allowing for too long a period for completion and thus producing procrastination and delay. In fact much was accomplished. A government of national unity was established. Constitutional changes permitted the south to establish a largely autonomous government and to retain its own army. At the same time, joint security units were created to patrol the border. Laws

◁ Sudanese march for separation from the north, Juba, Nov. 9, 2010. *Stefano De Luigi/VII/Network/Corbis*

were enacted to provide for national elections in 2010 and the self-determination referendum in 2011. Each step was the source of much hard work and not infrequent international involvement.

As the date for the self-determination referendum approached, it became clear that there was much that had not been done. Most important, the realization that the south would almost surely vote for secession only dawned upon the north and much of the international community in 2010. Partly this was due to mutual misconceptions about the CPA. For the government of Sudan, it was a blueprint for bringing the north and south together in a unified Sudan. Much of the rhetoric in the CPA pointed in this direction and the leadership of both sides was pledged to work for this goal. This was indeed the goal as well of the leader of the Southern Peoples Liberation Movement (SPLM) at the time, John Garang, who envisioned a new, more politically inclusive and diverse Sudan that would encompass Muslims and Christians, northerners and southerners, in the nation's national identity.

But events and lack of action took the process in a different direction. John Garang was killed in a helicopter accident in 2005, just months after the CPA was signed. Southern leadership thereafter became more focused on building the capacity and political foundation for independence of the south than on remaking the national political system. For its part, the government of Sudan did not open up the national political system as envisioned. The elections in 2010, which were expected to finalize this process, instead entrenched the National Congress Party (NCP) in power as opposition parties boycotted the election charging unfair practices and ultimately the rigging of the process. Despite there being a government of national unity throughout this period, there was no new identity promoted to describe a more multi-cultural and multi-religious nation. In the meanwhile, little was done to overcome the economic disparities between north and south. The latter continued to lack basic infrastructure and development, barely recovering from years of war and large-scale displacement of its population. By 2010, the prospects for the south not voting for secession were largely gone.

As the nation faced this reality, it became equally clear that few of the understandings regarding future economic, political, and security cooperation between north and south had been reached. One of the most acute was the future division of oil revenues on which both north and south depended. The south contains most of the oil fields, but the north has all the pipelines and infrastructure for export and refining, making cooperation a natural outcome but the details potentially very contentious. There were disputes over future borders, and competing needs of constituencies on either side that needed to be managed. Addressing any of these issues was made more difficult because of deep suspicion between the two sides about each other's motives that surfaced in almost every negotiating forum. Most worrisome therefore, as the time approached, was that the referendum would be blocked, delayed, or undermined by elements in the north, or preempted by precipitous action by the south such as a unilateral declaration of independence, threatening a renewal of civil war.

A Very Engaged International Community

From the beginning of the peace process, the international community was deeply involved. Sudan's civil war had cost two million lives, produced as many or more refugees and internally displaced people, cost billions in humanitarian assistance, and upset regional stability. There was thus considerable momentum for bringing the war to a close. In the United States, the war also had attracted politically influential religious and political groups. These included evangelical leaders, upset over the perceived oppression of Christians in the south by the Islamic north, and the Black Caucus in the U.S. Congress, alarmed over reports of slavery. President George W. Bush was thus early engaged on Sudan and in 2001 appointed a presidential envoy for the peace process, former Senator John Danforth. The lead in the early negotiations, however, came from the Intergovernmental Authority for Development (IGAD), an East African association of states, and in particular Kenya, whose General Lazaro Sumbeiywo would prove to be a most incisive and effective negotiator.

The breadth of international involvement was reflected by the number of signed witnesses to the CPA: Kenya, the U.S., the United Kingdom, Italy, Norway, the Netherlands, Uganda, Egypt, the IGAD Partners Forum, the Arab League, the United Nations, the European Union, and the African Union (AU). The CPA further provided for an internationally led Assessment and Evaluation Committee to monitor implementation of the agreement. The AU was later charged with overseeing negotiation of post-referendum issues and has created a High Level Panel made up of three former African presidents to undertake this task. The UN deployed a peacekeeping force and civilian contingent (UNMIS) to monitor security arrangements and to assist in the carrying out of the referendum and other aspects of the CPA. In addition, there are many formal and informal associations of international actors that have since become engaged on Sudan, e.g. the 'troika' made up of the U.S., UK, and Norway; the five permanent members of the UN Security Council who periodically address the Sudan issue; the Contact Group of nations not on the UN Security Council but having concern; a Consultative Group formed by the AU, to which it reports on the negotiations; a Policy Committee to oversee preparations for the self-determination referendum; and continuing attention from IGAD. There are also many individual special envoys for Sudan, from the U.S., UK, Norway, Sweden, the EU, China, Finland, Switzerland, South Africa, Russia, and other countries and organizations. All of this international attention, however, did not prevent the CPA process from teetering on the edge of failure by 2010.

The Darfur Factor

At about the same time as the final protocols were being negotiated between north and south, a rebellion broke out in 2003 in Sudan's western province of Darfur. The rebellion was partly a result of the peace process between north and south, in that people in Darfur—a politically and economically marginalized province—saw a division of political power and wealth being negotiated between north and south but leaving Darfur out. There were other deeper roots to the rebellion—years of drought that had aggravated competition for land between Arab nomadic tribes and African farmers, ethnic and tribal differences, and lack of real political power at the local and provincial level. The government of Sudan responded harshly. It armed Arab militias, the *janjaweed*, who proceeded to attack rebel areas, kill tens of thousands, rape, burn villages to the ground, and displace some two million people. The viciousness of these attacks, which seemed to take on a racial and ethnic character, led to charges of genocide, first by the U.S., later by the International Criminal Court (ICC). The ICC took the extraordinary step of indicting Sudanese President Omar Al-Bashir on charges of crimes against humanity, and war crimes in 2009, and issuing a warrant for his arrest on genocide charges in 2010.

The Darfur crisis had a major impact on U.S–Sudanese relations. Before the rebellion became a major focus of attention, the U.S. had conditioned its policy of normalizing relations with Sudan on completion of the north–south peace process. American officials indicated to the Sudanese government that if it signed the CPA and adhered to its provisions, the U.S. would take Sudan off the list of states sponsoring terrorism. It was a designation made in 1993 when the country hosted Osama Bin Laden and other terrorist organizations and reinforced in 1995 after a Sudan-based terrorist group attempted to assassinate Egyptian President Mubarak, but which by 2005 no longer reflected Sudanese policies or practices. With removal of that designation, sanctions could be removed and full diplomatic relations and economic cooperation could resume. Darfur changed all that. Despite the signing of the CPA and its implementation, the designation remained, and further sanctions related to Darfur were enacted by the U.S. Congress.

It is important to understand why Darfur became so important an issue in U.S. foreign policy. Partly it was timing. In 2004, think tanks, universities, and other organizations were preparing programs, seminars, and studies to look back ten years at the Rwanda genocide, to understand why the world had allowed it to happen. It was in this midst of all these programs that participants suddenly realized that another genocide was happening at that very time. If it was important to know why Rwanda was allowed to happen, it was even more urgent not to allow it to happen again, this time in Sudan. Darfur became a cause célèbre, drawing university students, religious organizations, human rights groups, and political leaders into a broad coalition to stop the war. Another factor was President George W. Bush. Early in his presidency he read a paper on the Rwanda genocide, and wrote in the margin, "Not on my watch." For Bush, this was a singular moral departure from the actions of the Clinton administration. Bush was further pressed on Darfur by the same evangelical organizations that had urged him to take leadership on the Sudan civil war, even though in this case, the Darfur crisis, both perpetrators and victims were Muslim. Finally, genocide produced a strong visceral reaction in the American public, with memories still alive from the Holocaust and deep guilt over the failure to act in Rwanda.

Jump-Starting the Peace Process

For several years after the outbreak of the fighting in Darfur, international attention vacillated between that crisis and the CPA, though most attention was focused on the former. However, in 2010, recognizing that time was running out on the CPA and that failure to complete it could ignite another civil war, there was a surge of Sudanese and international action to jump-start the lagging peace process. There would be numerous international meetings, high level statements, and visits urging the government of Sudan to adhere to the timelines and requirements of the CPA and to obtain its assurances of the same. The U.S. took several steps to build up its efforts. It increased the size of its presence in Juba, the capital of the south, with an emphasis on building the capacity of the southern government not only to administer basic services but prepare for likely independence. President Obama had early in his administration appointed a full-time presidential envoy for Sudan, retired General Scott Gration. The envoy team was later expanded with my appointment to head the north–south team in the presidential envoy's office and to be present nearly full time in Sudan. President Obama ordered a review of U.S. policy to iron out differences within the administration on how to proceed. He appeared personally at a UN meeting on Sudan in September with a strong speech on behalf of making the CPA work. Thereafter, high-level attention to Sudan within the White House would continue on a daily basis.

Concurrent with the more intense high level diplomatic campaign, there were three other overlapping processes that got under way. One was a more organized, formal negotiating structure. Developed under the guidance of the AU in May 2010, this structure divided the issues that had yet to be negotiated into four 'cluster groups' addressing respectively economic and natural resources, security, citizenship, and international treaties and other legal questions. The cluster groups were to address numerous technical questions. But many of these issues required political decisions. The latter would thus be addressed by a Lead Panel headed by chief negotiators for either side. As progress dragged within the cluster groups and other negotiating fora, the AU concluded in October that what was needed was a Framework Agreement that would set forth basic principles in each of these areas, as well as commitments to peace, pledges not to support groups aiming to destabilize each other, and other principles of cooperation between the future two states. Differences over Abyei and citizenship prevented the agreement from being signed before the referendum, but the AU publicized the provisions that had been agreed to reassure the public of the commitment of both sides to peace and future cooperation.

The second process was intensive work to plan for the referendum to take place on time. The Southern Sudan Referendum Act was not passed until 2009 and the Southern Sudan Referendum Commission (SSRC), established to carry out the referendum, was not put in place until July 2010. The SSRC was then bogged down throughout September 2010 by struggles over the appointment of a secretary general, dissension among commission members, threats by the chairman to resign, and lack of reliable financing. Given the voluminous decisions, the quantity of material to be designed, purchased, and printed, the thousands of registration and poll workers to be hired and trained, and a multitude of other tasks preliminary to carrying out a credible referendum, meeting the deadline seemed almost impossible. Many within Sudan and among the international community believed that postponement of the referendum was not only desirable but unavoidable. But any postponement threatened the peace. The south was determined on the date being honored. Moreover, any postponement, even justified on technical grounds, played into the hands of those who wanted for other reasons to delay if not scuttle the referendum. Finally, postponement would surely have taken away the sense of urgency needed to overcome the obstacles to getting the SSRC up and organized and able to carry out its job. The U.S. among others thus refused to countenance a delay, and worked to maintain international unity around holding the parties to that date. A major effort that combined frequent political pressuring by international actors, extensive technical support from the UN, the International Foundation for Electoral Systems and other sources of expertise, and courageous leadership by the SSRC chairman in the face of politically inspired criticism and threats, enabled the SSRC to confound all the predictions and be able to emerge on the dawn of the prescribed date ready and able to carry out the self-determination vote. One of the most serious threats to the peace had been overcome.

The third effort was a high-level process to secure the commitment of the parties to the CPA, and in particular to the holding of the southern referendum on time, January 9. In this context, the question had to be asked: what were the underlying concerns of each party that might lead them away from a peaceful process of separation? For the SPLM, the principal cause would be the fear that the north in the end would not allow the referendum to take place. That was leading the SPLM to actively examine alternatives, such as a unilateral declaration of independence, which would surely have threatened renewed war. The issues in the north thus became the most critical. The NCP had several deeply held reservations. One was the worry that once the south, which had considerable political support and sympathy in the west, was independent, the north would be abandoned and isolated by the international community. More conspiratorial, there was a belief in some quarters that the south would become a springboard for destabilization and regime change in the north, helped by foreign (meaning largely U.S.) powers. On the material level, there was quite legitimate concern over the loss of revenue from oil and the likelihood that continued economic sanctions, debt, and other factors would shut the north out for at least several years from the resources of international financial institutions, which would be needed to ease the shocks created by separation. Finally, the north feared that secession by the south could be followed by similar appeals from other regions of Sudan, whether Darfur, the east, or elsewhere, leading to the dismemberment of the country—or war to stop it. In brief, for some within the ruling party, implementation of the CPA would bring war, or economic collapse, or both. Why do it?

Many of these fears rested on the future relationship with the United States. There was a great deal of mistrust in the government's attitude toward the U.S. As noted above, the U.S. had placed Sudan on the list of states supporting terrorism, a designation that contained sanctions. In 2005, the U.S. promised to remove Sudan from the terrorism list and open the door to international assistance, if the government signed the CPA. However, these promises were withdrawn in the wake of the Darfur crisis. Sanctions were in fact added over Darfur. From the point of view of the NCP the U.S. had reneged, and any future such promises were considered untrustworthy. The ICC indictment of Al-Bashir added another impediment. Though not a member of the ICC, the U.S. took the position that the decision of the ICC should be honored and urged other countries to do so. In addition, the U.S. government would have no direct contact with Al-Bashir after the indictment (not an insignificant factor in trying to play our role in the CPA negotiations). Yet the U.S. was the key to opening the door to debt relief, international finance, and the restoration of Sudan to the good graces of the international community. In the eyes of many, improving the U.S.–Sudan relationship, assuring the NCP on these points, was thus critical to their having confidence in proceeding with the CPA.

Addressing this issue was not easy. U.S. sanctions were embedded in legislation as well as executive orders. Attitudes toward the Sudanese government in some quarters of the U.S. were quite negative, and some viewed any move toward lifting sanctions as a removal of needed pressure on the regime with regard to both the CPA and Darfur. Separating sanctions related to Darfur and the CPA also posed a problem, as the two situations were operating on different time lines: few expected a peace agreement in Darfur by the time of the southern referendum. Finally, there was some concern that putting too much emphasis on the U.S.–Sudan relationship was an easy way for the parties—and indeed the various international actors—to divert attention and effort from the difficult negotiating issue between the Sudanese parties. For the NCP it could succeed in winning concessions from the U.S. but not necessarily move it very far on the CPA, or simply encourage it to engage in a process of always asking more from the U.S. before it felt comfortable enough to return to the CPA. For the SPLM, putting emphasis on the U.S.–Sudan relationship allowed it to avoid making difficult compromises in the negotiations itself, shifting the responsibility for bringing along the NCP primarily to the U.S. In sum, the U.S.–Sudan relationship was an integral part of the process but it had to be kept in perspective. The CPA involved the most important decisions in Sudanese history since independence. Ultimately it was for the Sudanese to make the hard decisions in terms of their politics and their sense of the future of the country, not simply or primarily on the basis of the relationship with the U.S.

The U.S. first responded to the need to address the bilateral relationship by presenting Sudan with a new time line for normalization of relations. It included lifting some licensing restrictions on the import of agricultural equipment, began a process of consultation with the World Bank on debt relief for Sudan, and laid out a timeline for the process to remove Sudan from the terrorist designation and restoring full diplomatic relations, which was largely geared to both completing the CPA and satisfactory progress toward peace in Darfur. The offer was presented orally by presidential envoy Scott Gration in October 2010. The reaction was not positive. The timeline lacked specificity but implied that the earliest the terrorism designation could be removed was early 2012. Other forms of economic support were vague. Partners in the peace process as well as the NCP urged the U.S. to be more forward leaning. The U.S. followed up with a letter from the secretary of state reaffirming the offers delivered by General Gration. But this too did not satisfy.

In November, the U.S. refined its policy. In a letter to Senator John Kerry, chairman of the Senate Foreign Relations Committee, President Obama set forth a new timeline for normalization. Among the principal changes was that the process for withdrawing Sudan from the list of states sponsoring terrorism, a process requiring some six months, would begin as soon as the Government of Sudan accepted the results of the southern referendum. Further, provided Sudan met the requisite criteria under the law, the decision to remove it would be linked to satisfactory implementation of the CPA, no longer to Darfur. These changes from the original roadmap meant that the removal could come as early as July 2011. Other sanctions and trade restrictions could also be lifted by then, as well as active work with the World Bank and creditors on Sudan's need for debt relief.

Senator Kerry carried these new decisions to Sudan in early November and returned to Sudan a week later to reinforce the message. President Obama took some criticism in the U.S. for delinking the terrorism designation from Darfur, but the message conveyed to the Sudanese parties was that the CPA was of utmost importance and the U.S. was serious about normalization in its wake. Nevertheless, the U.S. warned that any serious deterioration in the situation in Darfur would affect the readiness of the administration and Congress to take these newly outlined steps. While no one in the NCP applauded the new U.S. offer, attention seemed to shift back to the issues at hand in Sudan.

Addressing the Most Critical Issues

The peace process divided the issues to be negotiated into pre- and post-referendum issues. But the line between them was not sharply defined. For example, how important was it to have agreement on the sharing of oil revenue before the referendum, or a firm agreement on citizenship, borders, or on currency arrangements, if the south voted for independence? Was agreement on general principles sufficient or did more specific agreements need to be put in place in order to give confidence to, in particular, the north and the population in general that the process would not be seriously detrimental, and to avoid situations that could produce conflict in disputed regions along the border? A paper prepared by the U.S. Institute of Peace in July 2010 suggested that a considerable degree of specificity in most of these areas was of high priority before the referendum. As the time for the referendum approached, the U.S. assumed that at least four matters needed to be agreed before January 9: sharing of oil revenues or at least general principles defining future cooperation in this sector; a solution for the special region of Abyei; citizenship; and border demarcation. We were to be surprised that few of these in the end were decided by the time of the referendum, as both parties gradually deferred most of these issues to post-referendum negotiations. Whether this was wise or not will be determined in the post-referendum period.

The U.S. had a special responsibility for helping find a solution for Abyei. American negotiators played a major role in the development of the Abyei Protocol within the CPA. Abyei is one of three regions in northern Sudan where the SPLM had active support and where parts of the civil war were fought. The question in the CPA negotiations was how to treat these regions in the context of a southern Sudan self-determination process. As the result of a hard-fought compromise, it was agreed that for Abyei, the Ngok Dinka and other residents of that region would be permitted to vote (also on January 9, 2011) whether to remain part of the north or become part of the south. For the other two—the states of Blue Nile and South Kordofan—there would be a process of 'popular consultations' that would make recommendations to define their future political relationship with Khartoum and for more inclusive governments at the state level. But this process would not (though this has not always been clear to the residents of those regions) allow for a vote to transfer to the south.

Abyei has become one of the most difficult and emotionally charged issues in the CPA. It has long been considered one of the most dangerous threats to the peace process. Indeed violence broke out there at the outset of voting in the southern referendum, requiring intensive diplomatic efforts to bring the situation under control. There is a long history to this issue that cannot be covered here. Suffice to say that the Ngok Dinka hold that Abyei is the land of the nine Ngok Dinka chiefs transferred to the north in 1905, and that the vote agreed on in the Abyei Protocol is primarily for the Ngok Dinka. It is assumed that they would vote to be reunited with the south. Abyei is also an area in which and through which clans of the Misseriya regularly migrate in the dry season for pasture and water for their cattle. The Misseriya, encouraged by the NCP, argue that they have special rights in Abyei and thus should have the right to vote in the referendum. Their numbers, however, could swamp the Ngok Dinka and thus the Ngok Dinka firmly oppose that proposition. While there are many traditional forms of cooperation between these two ethnic groups, there are deep sources of bitterness. Some of the Misseriya fought on the side of the northern government during the civil war and as late as 2008 attacked and burned down the city of Abyei. Other issues, such as charges of Misseriya kidnapping Dinka children and practicing slavery, color the attitudes of the Dinka. There have been several forms of arbitration. These reduced the size of the territory in question, but largely upheld the Ngok Dinka position on the nature of the referendum. These decisions have hardened the position taken by the Ngok Dinka and the feeling of the justice of their cause. But they have not moved the issue closer to resolution.

Abyei is not a large region and, contrary to media descriptions of it being 'oil rich,' its oil output is relatively insignificant. But it looms large in the political calculation of both north and south. On the Misseriya side, there have been promises by Al-Bashir to them about their rights to Abyei. Al-Bashir has a long personal history with this group. Moreover, the Misseriya remain a potent political and armed force that the NCP cannot afford to disappoint. Within the SPLM, there are high-ranking officials with deep family and personal ties to Abyei who insist that the issue is an important test of the SPLM's firmness in dealing with the NCP. Neither side feels it can afford to disappoint its constituencies. Abyei thus has loomed larger than it might in the CPA process and the hopes for peace.

By the middle of 2010, the issue was stuck. The NCP had not agreed to the formation of the commission needed to carry out the Abyei referendum, putting the referendum in doubt. In late September and early October, therefore, the U.S. attempted to mediate this issue in meetings in New York and Addis Ababa. Much of the focus in these meetings was on finding a formula for determining voter eligibility that would satisfy both parties and thus allow preparations for the vote to go forward. But following day after day of trial and error, sessions that went late into the night, it became clear that, as one participant put it, the referendum would become more a source of conflict than a peaceful resolution of the problem. We could not find any formula for allowing even some Misseriya to vote (e.g., those who spend at least eight months a year in Abyei and could thus be considered 'residents') that did not lend itself to possible rigging, and would therefore be acceptable to the Ngok Dinka. Indeed, however eligibility was defined to include both groups, registration on both sides could be challenged to such a degree as to paralyze the process and lead to violence. By the end of the Addis meeting, it seemed that a political solution, rather than a referendum, might be better. This could mean a presidential directive moving Abyei to the south (though this would not in itself be satisfactory to either the NCP or the Misseriya) or some compromise solution. The parties also concluded that the issue could perhaps be better addressed in the context of the negotiations on all other issues where trade-offs might be possible. Thus it went back to the overall negotiations under the AU.

It did not take long, however, for the AU to determine that an issue of such emotion, and of important political dimension to both sides, could not be decided by the negotiating teams. It could only be decided by the presidents—Al-Bashir, and Salva Kiir, the first vice president of the government of national unity but also president of the government of southern Sudan. The AU High Level Panel has put several ideas to the two presidents and they have met more than once to consider them. But they failed to reach agreement before the beginning of the southern referendum. The people of Abyei understandably feel angry and abandoned. This issue will have to be addressed early on after the southern referendum is completed.

If Abyei carries such emotion and political weight that it is understandable how hard a solution will be, it is not so clear why other issues have not progressed very far. Despite assumptions in the international community that oil revenue sharing and some of the other issues mentioned above would have to be resolved before the southern referendum, the parties failed to do so, despite numerous negotiating sessions. In the end, the NCP, which would have appeared to have the most at stake, did not insist on the resolution of any of them as a condition of the referendum getting under way. One can only speculate as to why this has happened. One factor is that up to only late November, there was hope in the north that the vote might lead to unity rather than secession. There may also have been hopes within the NCP that that referendum could still be stopped or delayed. That made negotiating on the basis of separation seem premature if not even unnecessary. Thus the NCP was not fully prepared in the waning days before the referendum to engage with these most important and far-reaching issues. Another theory is that both parties feel they will be in stronger positions on these issues after the referendum, when agreement will be essential. The SPLM will be dealing with them as a soon-to-be-independent nation. The NCP will still hold important cards to make that realization more or less difficult.

One issue that, like Abyei, should not remain long unsettled is citizenship. The NCP has taken a hard line, suggesting that all those eligible to vote in the referendum, should the outcome be secession, automatically become citizens of the new state of southern Sudan. This position raises serious questions of human rights, and given the time lag for the new southern state to establish citizenship laws and procedures, could lead to a situation of statelessness for southerners living in the north. It also creates more uncertainty among those southerners, perhaps one to two million, about their future safety and security in the north. Despite several statements by officials guaranteeing that regardless of the outcome of the referendum, these people's houses, jobs, and security will be protected, other statements, articles in the press, and a growing vindictiveness in some of the discussions have all created fear among this population.

A growing number of southerners in the north are thus moving to the south, creating a humanitarian problem. More than one hundred and fifty thousand have moved since August 2010. Many, after selling their belongings and leaving their jobs, have waited for weeks at roadsides or temporary campsites until transportation is available. There is also little for them when they arrive at their destinations. Thousands have ended up in the south in transit camps or temporary quarters dependent on international aid. Much of the responsibility for this situation lies with the government of the south, including individual governors, who have promoted this return but not provided sufficient transportation or integration when people arrive. But assurances from the NCP that there will be no loss of citizenship for southerners in the north, and allowing for a sufficiently long transition period for people to make personal decisions, will go a long way to avoiding panic and a larger humanitarian crisis.

The Way Forward

The success in carrying out the southern self-determination referendum marks a major milestone in the peace process. Now serious negotiations must begin on all the major issues that will define the future relationship between the two countries.

But even beyond the several post-referendum issues still to be resolved, the CPA faces further tests. One of the shortcomings of the CPA, from the beginning, is that the process has not been transparent. What that means is that it has been a process between two parties, and the international community. There has been little or no participation by civil society or even by opposition parties. The negotiations over the past year in particular have been largely opaque, with the details so complex and the structures so intricate that the public is not anywhere near informed about either the process or the outcome. The result is that while those directly involved, and those of us in the international community, have become increasingly optimistic that the future of two states can be managed cooperatively and without further war, that is not the feeling necessarily among the public. My meetings in the north with members of opposition parties, civil society, and youth, reveal a deep-seated pessimism. Fears that the CPA will surely lead to more war are prominent. Worries about economic dislocation, growing bitterness and recrimination between northerners and southerners, and political turmoil are readily expressed. None of these outcomes is inevitable, and most can be managed. But if the people of Sudan, perhaps mostly those in the north, feel this way then the CPA could fail due to lack of popular support and actions taken out of fear. Addressing these problems of public participation and anxiety must be high on the agenda of Sudan's leadership in the immediate post-referendum period.

The CPA was also supposed to usher in a period of political transformation in both north and south, with greater democracy and inclusiveness. That has not happened, and as the time for the referendum grew closer, those issues were put aside to deal with the decisions that existing leaders were in a position to make. These issues will now become more salient. Following the referendum, both north and south will need to develop new constitutions. There are large issues to be decided, on forms of government, methods of participation and inclusiveness, and human rights. These are matters in which the international community will be far less involved. They are domestic and sovereign decisions. But for the sake of both north and south, those decisions will need to be made carefully, with widespread public participation, and dedicated to a democratic outcome. In that way, each can emerge as a strong, viable, and stable state.

The views expressed in this article are those of the author and do not necessarily reflect those of the U.S. government.

Aida Seif El-Dawla Amr Khaled Nabil Fahmy

Essam El-Erian Esraa Abdel Fattah Hossam Badrawi

Amr Hamzawy Alaa Al Aswany Rami G. Khouri

The Cairo Review Interviews

Inside Egypt's uprising

Few imagined such a scene, such defiance: in Tahrir Square, a million Egyptians protested with a huge banner that read "PEOPLE DEMAND REMOVAL OF THE REGIME." Young activists used social media tools such as Facebook to organize the first protest on January 25, the country's Police Day. Eighteen days of mounting demonstrations later, with the country increasingly paralyzed, President Hosni Mubarak resigned after a thirty-year rule.

Mohammed Bouazizi, a twenty-six-year-old street vendor in the Tunisian town of Sidi Bouzid, is the one who lit the match that ignited the revolts against dictators throughout the Arab world. His self-immolation last December 17—after a government inspector confiscated his fruit and slapped him for trying to resist her authority—set off protests all over Tunisia and drove President Zine El-Abidine Ben Ali from power on January 14. Before long, uprisings also posed threats to longstanding regimes in Libya, Yemen, Bahrain, and Syria.

The Arab revolutions of 2011 are a turning point in Middle East history. Why did they occur? Why now? What comes next? In the *Cairo Review* Interviews, nine key figures give an inside look at the causes and effects of Egypt's uprising and discuss the challenges now facing the country and the region.

Cairo Review Q&A

FAITH AND HOPE IN EGYPT

Populist Muslim preacher Amr Khaled argues that economic development, religious coexistence, and international partnerships are keys to the country's future

Amr Khaled is an Egyptian preacher who reaches millions of Muslims through televised sermons on Arab satellite channels, and is the founder of development organizations such as Life Makers and the Right Start Foundation. Originally an accountant by training, Khaled began giving talks on religious topics in the mid-1990s to small groups gathered in private homes. Soon, his sermons in mosques were drawing thousands of Egyptians and his innovative development projects were getting results. Pushed out of Egypt by President Hosni Mubarak's regime, Khaled won legions of new followers with regional television programs that encouraged young arabs to improve their prospects. Khaled has been active in Egypt's transition and says he does not rule out running for president. The *Cairo Review*'s Ethar El-Katatney interviewed Khaled in Cairo on February 23, 2011.

CAIRO REVIEW: *What is your strongest memory of Egypt's January 25 Revolution?*
AMR KHALED: I think the word and concept of "peace." Of how much our youth did this revolution without any blood, how much they understood that Egypt has always been peaceful like that. This was a very important point. What our army and youth did in Tahrir is Egyptian civilization. My expectations were that there wouldn't be blood. It was a critical time though. Anything could go a different way. I'm so happy [about] what happened.

CAIRO REVIEW: *A specific moment that touched you?*
AMR KHALED: How the army dealt with me. The last day, it was not simple. [President Hosni] Mubarak's speech was unexpected and the people were so angry. At that time I was in Tahrir, so I met with one of the leaders of the army and he talked to me and said, "My sister [is] here, and my brother [is] here, I'm here. All of us are here. I will not shoot any of those [people], because all of them are my family." His words were very warm. And I believe that he was trying to say he, too, is one of the people.

CAIRO REVIEW: *How will Egyptians change?*
AMR KHALED: The expectations for their future became very, very high. People in Egypt now believe in freedom, democracy, youth empowerment. In 2006, I talked to the youth. I told them, please send me your dreams for the country, what you want [to see] in twenty years from now. In one month, I got 1.4 million replies. You know what was number one? "We want and need jobs." We need to respect ourselves, dedicate ourselves to work, create something.

CAIRO REVIEW: *Will dreams come true?*
AMR KHALED: To be honest with you, we need partners to create these huge numbers of jobs, after thirty years with no movement and the society the way it is now. We need to work. We need to move. We need to find solutions for problems. And the first challenge is to create jobs. So I believe we need partners. We need to feel that the West will not do injustice to us. There's a deep feeling that the West took our raw materials to the West, and left us. The Egyptian youth gives the West evidence that our quality is very good. We don't need [you] only to go to India or Singapore to start work and establish your programs and manufacturing. Come to Egypt. Give these youth opportunities. Open markets. We need buildings and projects. Give youth the opportunity to work.

CAIRO REVIEW: *How do you view the role that the United States played during the events?*
AMR KHALED: After the revolution, I'm not going to [make] speeches and talk about the past. Let's talk about the future. Now, the word hope for the Egyptian youth became very important. If no one extends their hands to help the youth in freedom and economic issues, these expectations they have will transfer to the opposite. It'll be depression. And I'm afraid if people don't reach out to the youth, there will be problems. They will be ready to go to the extremes. So for all of us, we need to talk about coexistence through projects. Not words. Projects.

CAIRO REVIEW: *Why did the youth revolt now?*
AMR KHALED: Actually, they're very patient. Thirty years is not a short time. It's a huge time. But we said it too many times, we have a problem. And no one listened and respected people. The average age is twenty-two. Can you imagine those people? No one respects them? No one gives them hope? So much energy, but nothing to do? No freedom. No jobs. No place to play even football. Where will my energy go? So we can't say "Why this day?" It was always going to happen. Many people were saying that.

CAIRO REVIEW: *What was the revolution for?*
AMR KHALED: Freedom. Just one word: freedom. Before January 25, for me to breathe freedom was impossible. I took the plane from Egypt to London to breathe the freedom. But now I can breathe the freedom in Egypt.

CAIRO REVIEW: *How have Egyptians changed?*
AMR KHALED: It changed [the] youth. For example, now religion is talked about [in] a different way. Not religion for religion. There's a huge difference. Before January 25, because there was nothing to do in society, they were talking about faith. At that time, I was talking about faith for development. Faith for faith could lead to extremism. But to talk about faith to make you build, create, do something for society, people wouldn't think like that. Now, people don't talk about faith just for faith. Faith to do something for Egypt.

CAIRO REVIEW: *What else?*
AMR KHALED: The world of coexistence changed since January 25. People would ask, "What do you mean by coexistence? Christians, Muslims? With the West?" Now it's an acceptable word, because in Tahrir, Muslims and Christians were together and had the same dream. Coexistence comes from us having the whole dream: the freedom of Egypt. But how can we use this energy and build a new dream? We need a new economic Egypt. Egypt could be one of the top ten in the world. The last thirty years, what was the dream of Egypt? Turkey has a dream, Israel has a dream, Malaysia has a dream. What does Egypt dream? Nothing in the last thirty years. Where do we start? The dream has to be to build Egypt. Develop this country. We deserve to be one of the best countries in the world. We need partners. Let's deal with the world. We don't want to be isolated any more.

CAIRO REVIEW: *What is your role in Egypt?*
AMR KHALED: I had this role before, but now it will be bigger, *insha'allah* (God willing), to empower civil society through many organizations, like Life Makers or others. To work for the sake of this country, to empower the youth. Because I believe the straight line to solve a lot of the problems in our country is empowering youth in civil society, to do something to build Egypt. That's my role now. And I will build it. A lot of youth organizations, Muslim and Christian, are working with me now. Ten million people are illiterate in Egypt. That can't be.

CAIRO REVIEW: *Did the Mubarak regime restrict your activities?*
AMR KHALED: You have to ask me? They stopped all my activities. They feared that civil society would be active or achieve something, the basics of democracy. They understood that. They knew I didn't talk about political issues. But what I was doing was the

root of democracy and politics. They tried to ban anything like that. My microfinance project was stopped in 2008, the 'Improving Lives Project.' The aim is to give projects, not money, to families in Upper Egypt, in Mansoura, in many places. On one condition: your kids have to go to school. Each family would have five youths to support them to do the project. The aim is not only the microfinance or the kids, but these youths would be leaders in the future. And the project was for seven thousand families which means [about] thirty-five thousand youths would work with them. After we started with that, two hundred families, 80 percent, succeeded. They started to work, and so on. The British Council gave us support to train the youth who would work with the families. And suddenly, in one day, they [the government] stopped this project. We tried, but they stopped us. So we went to other countries with our Egyptian youth, to do it in other countries, in Jordan, Algeria, Sudan, Yemen. We succeeded with one thousand families. And we felt so sorry we had to [do] this outside of Egypt and not [in] our country. But now they have all come back to establish this project with a huge number of families and youth, to work in Egypt.

CAIRO REVIEW: *Will you stay in Egypt?*
AMR KHALED: I'm back to Egypt. No more UK. I'm based here. We have two new projects, the literacy project for ten million people in five years, which we'll do with Vodafone. And the other project will be [the] 'Improving Lives Project.' We started this last week, not next month. We'll work on it for one year. The number of youths who will work with us as volunteers is about seventy thousand.

CAIRO REVIEW: *Are you going to get involved in politics?*
AMR KHALED: I believe I have a political role since I started, to make the civil society more active. Now I think that I have a deeper role in political issues. But in the right time. With the right image. I'll go to this role for sure, but step by step in the right way. It's too early to talk about this now. Leave it at the right time and come back to me at another time to make another interview with me and I'll tell you. Soon. Yes, I'm going to this role. But how much? When? Leave it to the right time.

CAIRO REVIEW: *Do you consider running for president?*
AMR KHALED: All the options are now open to us, it's a matter of choosing where we can be of most benefit. One way might be through the creation of a political party, but not a religious party. A party which is based on social development through politics. There's also the potential of taking other political steps that are bigger than creating a political party.

CAIRO REVIEW: *What are your priorities?*
AMR KHALED: Development, work. We have to pay the invoice of this revolution.

It's a great revolution. We did a great thing. All the world is watching. Egyptians are proud. But there is a great invoice [to be paid]. We need to create, work, make development. Egyptians have to prove, as we did with this revolution, we can make it different.

CAIRO REVIEW: *What are your concerns?*
AMR KHALED: Again we have to be patient. Thirty years. You want to change thirty years in five days or months? You need time. We need to support this economy. And to wait and be patient. It'll take time. We have to talk to the people and trust the country. Trust the economy. We have to give a message to the world: Come to this country. Invest in this country.

CAIRO REVIEW: *What else?*
AMR KHALED: The challenge now can be coexistence between Egyptians—Muslims and Christians. I'm not very worried, but I hope [coexistence] will stay very strong like the time of the revolution. This is one of my hopes and dreams in the future. But what worries me still is the economy. This is the only obstacle I see. I believe and trust the army. I don't think any threat will come [from] the army. And after five months, there will be civil society. Some people say, "They're not ready for democracy." How can you say something like that? All the world said, "We should take notes from Egyptians!"

CAIRO REVIEW: *How do you move from a revolution to a democracy?*
AMR KHALED: My son is ten years old. He was talking to me yesterday about the constitution. Can you imagine? Ten years old. We have to put the constitution in our houses. Kids, youth, must talk about our rights, our roles in society. Everyone's talking about [that]. No one is talking about sports. I mean, I believe in football, but now people are talking about politics. It's a new world in Egypt.

CAIRO REVIEW: *Who would be a good president?*
AMR KHALED: I believe that there are many people in Egypt, but no one would talk, in the past. They didn't have a chance. Most of these people, you will find them, starting in the next months, talking to the people. So I believe that we have numbers of people. Not a few. Many. They will start to take their role. It's too early to say this name or this name. Wait for two or three months. I know a lot of them. In the past, we were worried about minorities talking on behalf of the majority. Like the Muslim Brothers, and so on and so on. Now all society became active. We're not worried about any minorities pushing all over the society. Many names mean the right democracy. And everyone in this society in Egypt can think and listen. Many opinions.

CAIRO REVIEW: *What are you thoughts about the Muslim Brotherhood?*
AMR KHALED: We're talking about a civil country and government. Religion is very important for the people in this area of the world. But faith for what? Faith for development would be helpful for the future. I believe we are talking about faith, and faith for all, Muslims and Christians. Faith can encourage and motivate the people to build a country. This is what I think will be the future and role of faith.

CAIRO REVIEW: *How does Islam affect democratic practice?*
AMR KHALED: The model I choose to put is faith for the sake of the country. Maybe some people have another model. And maybe I don't accept it, or find it's not the right time for the country. But I think my model is needed right now. But I told you, after the revolution, the majority became active and positive. In the past you had to choose [between] government or Muslim Brotherhood. And people don't like the government. But now a lot of players have new ideas, good ideas. All people want everything to change. I don't think there will be a fear. You can go now to the Internet and read what Egyptians and youth are saying. They've changed. Revolution is not a simple word. It did a lot to change the minds. Especially the youth. They're ready to change very quickly.

CAIRO REVIEW: *You view on the Muslim Brotherhood?*
AMR KHALED: During the time of the revolution, they didn't try to do anything against the mainstream of the people. They were part of Egyptian revolution and they didn't try to take it for themselves. And at same time, they said "We won't run for presidential elections." I think they won't do anything against the sake of Egypt. This is in the past. Now, wait and see. This is a very critical [issue], so let's see. But there's no fear. People became very positive. I can't tell you that now. Wait and see what will happen. I was in Tahrir Square. Supporting youth through my Facebook page. More than two million youth followed us on this page. We have to listen and accept what our youth want. This is their freedom and country. We have to support it.

CAIRO REVIEW: *How do you label yourself?*
AMR KHALED: I'm a reformer. My role is of a reformer using faith, using and talking about hope. My role is to give hope and big dreams. To talk to [young people] about their dreams in the future. Send me your dreams. Hope and dream. I want to believe in them and give them. I have a message for the Arab youth, especially now in Tunis, Algeria, Yemen, Libya. All of us have to respect your dreams: you are a treasure. You're the treasure— not the oil, the gas. You have to dream and think. You will change your country and make a better future. And at the same time, you have to accept others. My message to Arab youth, you need others. You need coexistence. Extend your hands.

Cairo Review Q&A

"I Want a Democratic Egypt"

"Facebook Girl" Esraa Abdel Fattah appeals to members of her generation to become active in political parties for the sake of rebuilding their nation

Esraa Abdel Fattah, twenty-nine, is a coordinator for the Egyptian Democratic Academy, a nongovernmental organization promoting democracy and human rights. Born the year after Hosni Mubarak became president, she was an unlikely heroine in the fall of Mubarak's thirty-year regime. She started as a campaign volunteer with the opposition Al-Ghad party, whose leader, Ayman Nour, was later jailed by the regime for three years. She rose to prominence in 2008 as co-founder of the April 6 Movement, a group organized on Facebook to support industrial strikes, and became a leading activist in the January 25 revolution. The *Cairo Review*'s Lauren E. Bohn interviewed Abdel Fattah in Cairo on February 27, 2011.

CAIRO REVIEW: *How did you become an activist?*
ESRAA ABDEL FATTAH: I started my activism in 2005, during the presidential election and when Ayman Nour was arrested. I feel that I should be involved in the political life. I wanted to send a message to the government that you can't arrest anyone who just says their opinion. I wanted to say my opinion. I'm not happy with being silent about all the corruption around me. I started to be an activist through the Al-Ghad party because I thought it was a young party, caring about the young people, and the majority of the members of this party were my age. I like [Ayman Nour's] courage. I like that he insists on his rights, insists to be active to send a message to the people that the president should be changed, not just one person this whole time.

CAIRO REVIEW: *You were detained for two weeks after the April 6 campaign. Then you made a public statement renouncing activism. Why?*
ESRAA ABDEL FATTAH: Yes, my mother told me, in front of a lot of cameras here, that you should be away from activism. At this moment, I can't say no to her. Yes, I will be away, yes mom, but after a while I can't be away. I needed some time to refresh my mind, establish my thoughts and then I returned to activism. I returned

to Al-Ghad party for some time, then I left the party in 2009. I was involved in online activism, saying my opinion through the social media. I created a group calling for a general strike in Egypt.

CAIRO REVIEW: *How have your views about activism changed over the years?*
ESRAA ABDEL FATTAH: In 2005, I had a low profile. After 2008, I found myself as one who sends the message to people, "We can change our country, we can change Egypt to what we want." I think it's better to be an independent activist. I think the change should be through the system of elections so I became involved in a campaign called "My Vote is My Right." This campaign is specialized in changing the election system. Then, I had a very big role in monitoring the election. I was a consultant with a program on how to use the social media, and Google Earth, in monitoring elections. I worked in this project for a year, then after that we worked in the [Mohamed] ElBaradei campaign. I supported his right to be a presidential candidate. I also participated in all campaigns for Khaled Said [a young Egyptian killed in police custody in Alexandria in 2010], and the last [campaign] is the revolution on 25 January.

CAIRO REVIEW: *How did you participate during the eighteen days of the revolution?*
ESRAA ABDEL FATTAH: Before the revolution, I publicized the event on Facebook. I was in the Al Jazeera Forum, and this forum is live, and I called on all Egyptian people to say we refuse to celebrate Police Day because policemen are killing people. I recorded a video for about two minutes in this forum, to encourage people to join us in the street. In the days before the revolution, I specialized in how we can raise the money for the logistics for the things we need, and what we can write in the signs we used in this revolution. In the eighteen days, I helped using Facebook and Twitter to provide coverage for what happened in Tahrir Square. I participated in a lot of TV shows to say my opinion.

CAIRO REVIEW: *What was the role of social media?*
ESRAA ABDEL FATTAH: Yes, I think this social media had a great role. We used this tool to organize people, to prepare what to say, when to move, when to stop. We used social media to organize ourselves in a very active way. To publicize the event the way we want, and to make coverage for the events that happened in the street. And when we broadcast what happened, at the same time we encouraged them to join us in the street.

CAIRO REVIEW: *What sparked the January 25 revolution?*
ESRAA ABDEL FATTAH: I think the first thing is the revolution in Tunisia. It helped us to think, "We can change." This is the energy of what we felt at this time. Then, we

tried to rethink our demonstrations. They were not active and always the same people. We thought that now we should go to the other streets and to walk in them so the numbers increase and we can meet and arrive in the main square. I think these two things—rethinking our previous demonstrations and the Tunisian revolution—are the energy for us to make the 25 January revolution.

CAIRO REVIEW: *What made you frustrated and so angry?*
ESRAA ABDEL FATTAH: We have a lot of bad things in Egypt. We don't have anything good before 25 January. We have corruption in every field. We have corruption in elections. We have no democracy, no freedom of expression. All my colleagues are in prison and I was in prison, just for expressing my opinion on a Facebook page. I see the raising of prices without any consideration for raising peoples' incomes. There is no discipline in any place in Egypt. The system of punishment is not found in any institution or any ministry. No one can say what you did was wrong and what you did was right. Everyone just does whatever they want, without any reference to the law or the constitution. The corruption before 25 January, you can find it in every place in Egypt, I think the cause of the revolution. You make a lot of pressure with what happened to Ayman Nour, the pressure of raising prices, the bad education system, the bad economic system, all these pressures are on the people on 25 January.

CAIRO REVIEW: *What was the role of the youth?*
ESRAA ABDEL FATTAH: The youth started the energy for this revolution. But after 25 January, all the other people with different ages participated in this revolution.

CAIRO REVIEW: *Who are your leaders?*
ESRAA ABDEL FATTAH: No one can be a leader for this revolution. We started calling for revolution and all Egyptians participated in different ways. There is no leader that says we should go to Tahrir Square and we should leave Tahrir Square. The people led this revolution automatically, without anyone saying anything.

CAIRO REVIEW: *Who do you favor in a presidential election?*
ESRAA ABDEL FATTAH: I support ElBaradei to be the president in the next election. I think he is the suitable one for this period. But I care more for the system for how we choose. I don't care about the person. I care about the system.

CAIRO REVIEW: *What do you want for Egypt?*
ESRAA ABDEL FATTAH: I want a democratic Egypt. I want to feel that the people

who come in the parliament are chosen by the people, not by corruption. I want to say that the president is coming by the will of Egyptians and he will leave by the will of Egyptians.

CAIRO REVIEW: *What are Egypt's priorities now?*
ESRAA ABDEL FATTAH: Security returned to the streets, the change of the government, the punishment of all the old people who made corruption or killed people in the revolution. And the system of elections.

CAIRO REVIEW: *What will be your role in the next year or so?*
ESRAA ABDEL FATTAH: I will participate in a party. I will participate in a liberal party. I will be I think one of the leaders of this party. Maybe I can run in the parliamentary election.

CAIRO REVIEW: *What problems should be addressed immediately?*
ESRAA ABDEL FATTAH: I think after the transition period, we need a new constitution, a democratic one valid for the democratic country.

CAIRO REVIEW: *Did you see the revolution coming?*
ESRAA ABDEL FATTAH: I felt what happened on 25 January will come, I know this day will come, but I don't expect it will be on 25 January. I just think this day will come before the [presidential] election in September.

CAIRO REVIEW: *How do you feel now?*
ESRAA ABDEL FATTAH: I am proud to be Egyptian. But I am worried about achieving all our list of demands after the departure of Mubarak. I am worried about how we can achieve them.

CAIRO REVIEW: *Before the revolution, was it difficult to teach young Egyptians about democracy?*
ESRAA ABDEL FATTAH: Yes. Some people have a good background about politics and they wanted to participate. Others said, "There is no space to participate in political life and no democracy. Mubarak will stay and his son will come after him."

CAIRO REVIEW: *Did the government prevent you from establishing your democracy organization?*
ESRAA ABDEL FATTAH: No, but when we were making some events, we found that the regime canceled them.

CAIRO REVIEW: *How do you view the position that the U.S. government took during the revolution?*
ESRAA ABDEL FATTAH: In the first part of the revolution, I was disappointed by the reaction of the U.S.: "We trust the regime and we want to establish stability in Egypt." I was disappointed. But when they saw that the people had more power than Mubarak, the U.S. started to change to support the people.

CAIRO REVIEW: *What is the view of young Egyptians toward issues like the Israeli–Palestinian conflict, the Egyptian–Israeli peace treaty, the influence of Hizballah's Hassan Nasrallah or Iranian President Mahmoud Ahmadinejad?*
ESRAA ABDEL FATTAH: We don't care about all this in this revolution. We didn't care about what Hassan Nasrallah said or what the other people said in Iran, because we are very pissed about what happened in Egypt. We talk about what Mubarak said and what Mubarak did. We think they have no influence in Egypt. They just talk, they just mention something for the people, they have no influence on what happened in Egypt.

CAIRO REVIEW: *How do you address these other issues?*
ESRAA ABDEL FATTAH: I think this is not the time for this. We have no stable situation in Egypt. We care about what's inside and don't find time to talk about the foreign relationship between us and the others. This time will come after we choose a president. Then we will talk and say what the Egyptian role is in these situations, but there is no time for that now.

CAIRO REVIEW: *What is your message to young people who look up to you as a role model?*
ESRAA ABDEL FATTAH: I advise them, not only after 25 January, that we should participate in all political affairs in Egypt. We should participate not only by talking, but by actions. We should be a part of political parties. We should participate in elections. We should have the courage to say there is corruption, and the courage to stop everything wrong we see. We should participate in all fields in Egypt and then the people will build the new Egypt.

CAIRO REVIEW: *Are people ready for that?*
ESRAA ABDEL FATTAH: We need time to make them more aware. We need time for workshops, for training on what policy means, what elections mean.

Cairo Review Q&A

"I DIDN'T SEE IT COMING"

Former National Democratic Party Secretary General Hossam Badrawi tells how the Tahrir revolution looked from inside the regime

Hossam Badrawi has served as a member of the Egyptian parliament and is a professor of medicine at Cairo University. He joined the ruling National Democratic Party in 2000, telling the media that he hoped to play a role in reforming Egypt from within the system. He became a member of the NDP's Policy Secretariat, headed by Gamal Mubarak, and in February 2011 amid mass protests against the Egyptian regime he replaced Safwat El-Sherif as NDP secretary general. He held the job for only four days before resigning from the post and the party. *Cairo Review* Managing Editor Scott MacLeod interviewed Badrawi in Cairo on February 21, 2011.

CAIRO REVIEW: *What happened in Egypt?*
HOSSAM BADRAWI: It's a revolution. It changed the status of Egypt and it will definitely affect the future. Unexpectedly, it is the middle-class, educated people that made the change. Other sectors of the society have joined in. Some sectors are benefiting more. But the major move of the people: it is much more effective than in the revolution of 1919. And definitely more credible than 1952, because it's from the people, not the army. Egypt is making history for the Middle East.

CAIRO REVIEW: *Looking at it from the inside, did you see it coming?*
HOSSAM BADRAWI: I didn't see it coming in that way. But the ceiling of my expectations was much less than what happened. In 1990, we were many people working for reform in Egypt from outside the government. The structure that had all of us was the New Civic Forum, led by Dr. Said El-Naggar. Some of us decided we can make the change from inside. I represented that group. Others decided to make the change as opposition. Some others stayed independent. But there is a network between us. Because we are looking for liberal thinking. We were all for a free economy, democracy, human rights. We decided to play different roles from different positions.

And, I used to tell my friends, the most difficult position is mine. It is easy to be an opposition from outside. It's much more difficult on the inside and keep your credibility by saying what you want to say. And bear in mind the fact that you're not implementing what you want.

CAIRO REVIEW: *What did you think would happen?*
HOSSAM BADRAWI: I thought by accumulated pressure, we could change Article 77 [in the constitution] and have limitations on the president's terms, and change Article 76 for the way the elections can be done. And at the same time, remove the emergency [law] situation. And make the changes that implement human rights issues in the right structure. There's a document coming from me as a responsible person for the UPR, the Universal Political Review, of Egypt in early 2010 [and] stated all these facts. I presented it to the United Nations despite the fact that I was in the NDP, which put me in conflict with the party at the time. If Article 77 was going to change and limit the president's term, I was going to be so happy. I thought it would be an opening for everything, for political reform. I would have been satisfied if I'd seen limitation of terms and implementation of human rights. Obviously, what happened [in the revolution] is much more than that.

CAIRO REVIEW: *And you didn't see it coming?*
HOSSAM BADRAWI: No, I didn't see it coming. I expected change, but I didn't see it coming. Not that way. I thought with the change of the president, the whole country would be changed. I thought [President] Mubarak should have announced he wouldn't run again. I was advocating that. I thought by just changing that, most changes would happen by default.

CAIRO REVIEW: *So you didn't see a popular protest movement coming up to effect change?*
HOSSAM BADRAWI: No, I didn't see it that way. I didn't expect the middle-class people to come together that way and be that effective. It was a good surprise.

CAIRO REVIEW: *Was that a common perception in the party, the president and others didn't see the wave coming?*
HOSSAM BADRAWI: I think so. I realized on the first day, some people didn't realize what was happening even at the time it was happening. Every response from the president was too little too late, all the time. As I was given the post to direct the NDP in those four days, I had access to him and the group around him. I didn't have it before. I didn't have it afterwards. But during that time, I realized that they are responding

always too late and too little. They don't evaluate the magnitude of what's happening. My role in those four days was to open everyone's eyes, that this reality has to be respected and that the president has to step down now. That "now" was not accepted, day after day after day.

CAIRO REVIEW: *Were you able to say that personally to the president?*
HOSSAM BADRAWI: Personally, yes, the first day I met him. I told him he has to respect his promises to the people by amending the constitutional term [limits] and move all his authority to his vice president. I thought this is going to be more constitutional and that has to be done in the way people believe it. So he has to be clear about that, that he is not going to practice his presidency, except for one issue: to call for the referendum on the constitution, and that people should see and believe that is happening and it should be real. The delivery of his speeches did not give the impression that this was real. That was the defect. Until now I still think that moving the authority to vice president and his stepping aside from the presidency would have led the country in a more constitutional way than what is happening now.

CAIRO REVIEW: *Did you mean that he resign, or hand over power?*
HOSSAM BADRAWI: Hand over the power to the vice president, and to respect the constitution, so that he would have only one role, calling for the referendum. His role will be only one thing to do.

CAIRO REVIEW: *But he should remain as president?*
HOSSAM BADRAWI: Remain as president outside of the circle of authority. So he passes all his authority, gives it to the vice president, and moves geographically somewhere else, so he is not part of making decisions. And have things done constitutionally, and call for early elections once the constitution was amended. That was my opinion that I told him face to face.

CAIRO REVIEW: *Did you ever just ask him to completely resign the presidency, as he did on February 11?*
HOSSAM BADRAWI: No, I didn't advise that. But every day that passed, I realized even the advice [I gave him] wouldn't be accepted [by the revolution]. On the last day, I told him that even if you take my advice now, it can be successful only 10 or 15 percent. You're late. People do not believe there's an honest desire to step away and have the constitution be amended, and elections to be done as early as possible. That was the safest way the country can go, in my opinion.

CAIRO REVIEW: *What was President Mubarak's reaction to that advice? Did he deny there was a problem?*
HOSSAM BADRAWI: Actually not. We had meetings more than three times. On Wednesday, I was not giving him advice. I was giving my statement as the secretary general of the ruling party, a position he assigned me to have two days before. I told him that from the meetings I had from different political parties and with the people in Tahrir—I had many people there with the young people—that my political understanding was that the problem isn't in taking the action. The challenge is that they don't believe that you are taking the action. It wasn't advice. It was a request. And when the request was not met the way we agreed upon, I resigned.

CAIRO REVIEW: *He disagreed with the request?*
HOSSAM BADRAWI: No, he agreed. He understood it. He brought his legal people to make his statement on Wednesday. When I left, I was expecting him to give his statement on Wednesday, and he didn't give it. So it was clear to me that somebody else had called him. On Thursday, I made another attempt, that he should give his statement. It is already coming to be late. He told me that he is going to give his statement by the end of the day. Then they waited and waited until 10 p.m. or something like that. The statement came in my opinion with the worst delivery, in spite of the fact that it has all the content. But the delivery was not believable to the people. At that level I was cut from communication. I could not be part of the decision making anymore. I waited. I tried to communicate and couldn't. So I resigned.

CAIRO REVIEW: *In the speech, he followed the advice?*
HOSSAM BADRAWI: Yes, it followed my advice. But we had an agreement that the core of his speech should be that he was giving away his authority, clear cut. This was said in three seconds. If you look somewhere, you might not even have noticed. The delivery of the speech was not coinciding with the meaning. He started talking about himself and gave the impression that he is there. This was a big mistake. He gave his sharing of the grief of the young people who died. This was a request of the young people I met and I asked for. He separated between the revolutionary and the criminal acts. That was a request, that he has to give it to the people. But at the end of the day, if history looks at the core without the delivery system, then you realize he gave away his powers, and gave the order for constitutional amendments. So he's not needed as a president anymore, only to call for the referendum. He didn't say that, he didn't press on that, he didn't give the impression that this was the situation. The content was there, but the meaning and understanding was not there.

CAIRO REVIEW: *He was not in denial about what was happening in Tahrir? He had already dismissed the leader of the party and even Gamal Mubarak.*
HOSSAM BADRAWI: That was my request, by the way. That was my request. When he assigned me as secretary general, I said everyone has to resign. I have to have full authority to reform the party.

CAIRO REVIEW: *So you think he was trying to remain part of the system, not to exit?*
HOSSAM BADRAWI: I think the circle around him was putting him to that situation. I had the feeling that he really wanted a constitutional path. And that he's stepping down anyway, anytime. But again, the decision and timing is part of the formula. And I think they were not—his advisors—were not helpful to let him take the right action at right time.

CAIRO REVIEW: *Why?*
HOSSAM BADRAWI: I'm not sure, but probably they were in denial more than him.

CAIRO REVIEW: *Why did the president finally resign on the Friday?*
HOSSAM BADRAWI: I saw it coming. After his speech on Thursday, and what happened Thursday night and Friday, it was clear that it is the point of no return. I think he had no choice.

CAIRO REVIEW: *Did the army go to him and say he had to step down?*
HOSSAM BADRAWI: All theories are possible. I was cut completely after I left the president's house on Thursday. On Thursday evening and Friday, I was like you, listening to news and seeing it on TV. I was cut. I was not connected. I tried but I couldn't. I came on TV [and resigned]. The only way for me was to give a statement to the BBC so it becomes public. At the end of the day, the publicity is the reality.

CAIRO REVIEW: *Why do you think the revolution happened?*
HOSSAM BADRAWI: I think the reaction of the police was one of the factors to create the movement. Because the excessive use of violence was part of the accumulation of other people to come in. At one level, the fear has gone. The numbers made it possible for the fear of the security forces to go away. Everybody underestimated the capacity of the youth to represent their opinion. There was underestimation of that capacity by the whole society, even by their parents, who joined them later.

CAIRO REVIEW: *What led to January 25?*
HOSSAM BADRAWI: It was the accumulation. I think it's the human integrity and the human rights, more than anything else. It was not those who do not have

employment. It was people with good employment in the streets. I think it was humiliation. I call it chronic anger, a chronic state of anger. In medicine, the chronic situation, you get adapted to the pain until it becomes acute. The acute exacerbation made all chronic anger come up. Part of it was, in my opinion, the way the state was dealing with the people, humiliating them in everyday activities. The relationship of the individuals with the police. They way you get your services from the state, from the cabinet, from the public officials. Everything had to do with whether you have a *wasta* (connections) or pay a bribe. Everybody was telling their kids, "If a policeman stops you, don't argue." These situations were elevating the dissatisfaction and anger. Not acute enough to revolt, but it's there. Trigged by something, everybody came together.

CAIRO REVIEW: *What was the trigger?*
HOSSAM BADRAWI: The excessive use of violence within the police. Khaled Said [a young Egyptian killed in police custody in Alexandria in 2010] was part of it. And the excessive use of violence in Tahrir on the first day. On the first day everyone was calling for freedom and justice. It was not about food or unemployment. That was a collective request of everyone. As they got larger and larger, the line of fear has gone. And then with the late response, and the little response, objectives went higher. If on January 25 the president had come out to the people and said, "I'm dissolving the government and not running [for re-election]," probably everyone was going to be happy. As you go day after day, and people get hurt and die, and you are not seeing the leader of the country coming to talk to the people for three days, this was cumulative bad management of the crisis. It made the chronic stage into an acute stage.

CAIRO REVIEW: *Was the "succession issue" a factor? The 2010 parliamentary elections? The Gamal Mubarak question?*
HOSSAM BADRAWI: I add it as a factor to the chronic anger. There were no clear-cut announcements [about Gamal Mubarak] that people could protest against. But it created the feeling that something weird was being cooked. The president should have come clearly and said that he wasn't going to run, and that no one from his family was going to run, to give that kind of satisfaction. The parliamentary election in 2010 was another important factor. In a meeting after the election, in the party they were announcing we had the largest victory any party had. I raised my hand and said, from a limited party point of view, it might be true. But from a political point of view, I think this is the largest defeat we've had. Because if you do not have opposition in the parliament, you will have them in the streets. And if it was in my hand, I would definitely have worked harder for the opposition to have them represented in the parliament. And I had that conflict with the administration, because I was sure that

playing alone is not in the benefit of the country. And having the parliament unilaterally ruled was not going to be accepted by anyone. In spite of the fact that they had so many proofs that they won fair and square against the Muslim Brotherhood. It was a disaster and added to the chronic anger.

CAIRO REVIEW: *What was your assumption about Gamal Mubarak's intentions?*
HOSSAM BADRAWI: I was there for eight years, and this was never discussed between me and him, never raised as an issue in the party. But actions give different impressions. I don't know if there was a smaller circle talking about that and I wasn't a part of it. His presence and his leading of the party and his appearances and visits to different areas of the country, gave the impression that he's politically portraying himself. He never talked about this with me, maybe with others. I once told him in the party, that the relationship of the party with the government is not [correct], because if it was [correct], it should not depend on the president or the son of the president. It should depend on the dynamics of politicians. There was so much implementation of policies that we worked out that was not done. And I cannot make any difference. It is always going back to the president, whether he gives instructions to the government or not. It is all a relationship between the government and the president's house.

CAIRO REVIEW: *The NDP is not a real party?*
HOSSAM BADRAWI: It was a real party, but very centralized. There were very good people. Excellent policy papers were done with lots of efforts from intellectuals and politicians, learning from the experiences of other countries. But that stops here. Whether that was being taken seriously by the government was something else.

CAIRO REVIEW: *In the upper levels of the NDP, was it your assumption that Gamal was being prepared to become president?*
HOSSAM BADRAWI: Yes. It was an assumption, yes.

CAIRO REVIEW: *Was this ever an issue to raise that this was not a good idea, and could damage the president and the country?*
HOSSAM BADRAWI: Yes. But sometimes when you say that to the person, he says "No, I'm not intending," then the discussion becomes "Who said I want to do that?" And the president says "My son is just helping me." The discussion stops.

CAIRO REVIEW: *What was going through your mind when you saw the NDP headquarters being burned?*
HOSSAM BADRAWI: Actually, I wasn't only looking at the NDP being burned,

but all police stations being burned down across the country. And all prisons being opened for prisoners to go away. And the NDP locations in eleven governorates being burned, and synchronized in the same way: we get in, steal contents, burn papers, get the hard disks of the computers. I don't think this was the revolution in Tahrir. It was much more organized than that. You have to think that there is a mastermind. I cannot assume [who is responsible] because I don't have any evidence. Don't tell me people in the streets going for their dignity and freedom organized that. It cannot be. We have to see who is going to benefit. The story did not come to the final chapter. So let's see who will take power, and then we'll know who's the beneficiary.

CAIRO REVIEW: *What happens next?*
HOSSAM BADRAWI: I want a transition to take place in a secular, civil structure. However, if the parliamentary elections are being held early, I think Egypt won't come to a stable situation for a long time. If we do not give time for parties coming out of the revolution to establish themselves and be a part of the coming elections, we're not giving them equal opportunity with others who are already structured and ready for those elections. The army has played a neutral role. I think they're overwhelmed with responsibility they are not trained to do. And I believe they would like to pass authority as fast as possible. But I hope "as fast as possible" doesn't affect the right decision. We have fragmentation now. We need one and a half to two years.

CAIRO REVIEW: *Would the Muslim Brotherhood win the election?*
HOSSAM BADRAWI: They would be the only party inside the parliament. The NDP isn't there. So other members would be individuals, independents running without a cover.

CAIRO REVIEW: *Is the NDP finished?*
HOSSAM BADRAWI: No, I don't think so, but I think it needs years to recover with new branding. It used to depend on being a part of the ruling structure, so it lost its magnet for people who want to become part of the government. But it is still the only structure that exists other than the Brotherhood. The NDP will need three or four or five years of working hard to change the image. There's a very negative impression. You have to rebrand.

CAIRO REVIEW: *Is the political role of the Mubaraks in Egypt now over?*
HOSSAM BADRAWI: Yes, it is.

CAIRO REVIEW: *Does Gamal Mubarak have any chance to be part of the rebirth of the NDP?*
HOSSAM BADRAWI: No. I don't think he has any role in the future.

CAIRO REVIEW: *What are your plans?*
HOSSAM BADRAWI: I'm just listening to people, analyzing, and giving my fair opinion. I meet with all political sectors. And I think in the turbulence that exists, people have to wait and see. If there is a party that can come from down up, I'll join.

CAIRO REVIEW: *How has Egypt fundamentally changed?*
HOSSAM BADRAWI: There is great opportunity for Egypt to move forward politically. It will affect the economy. I'm an optimistic person by nature. I see the opportunity there. But there are huge risks. If we fall into linear thinking that does not accept differences of opinion—either a military or a conservative religious one—neither would be best for the country.

CAIRO REVIEW: *There's a risk the military might take control completely?*
HOSSAM BADRAWI: I don't know. They are there now.

CAIRO REVIEW: *You're worried about the Brotherhood?*
HOSSAM BADRAWI: My intellectual structure is to be an open person, respect diversity, and accept differences in opinion. I have nothing against a woman president, or a Coptic Egyptian president, so long as it's through a democratic process. I definitely would like to see citizenship rights regardless of any religious belief. I see that that path might not be the path of the Muslim Brotherhood for the time being. Yet, they have good things to offer. This is the only thing that makes me worry. I have so many friends in the Muslim Brotherhood, good people and excellent people. They have good intentions. They should be part of the political scene, but they shouldn't impose their style on me.

CAIRO REVIEW: *Should the future system hold the former regime accountable?*
HOSSAM BADRAWI: That worries me very much, the fact that everything is being taken now by impressions. The rule of law should be the rule of law. We cannot accuse any person and accuse and incriminate and judge at the same time. That's very scary. I'm afraid of a sort of McCarthyite attitude, that once you're different in opinion, you'll be taken hostage by the fact you're different. As if we are moving from one kind of dictatorship to another kind of dictatorship.

NARRATING THE REVOLUTION

Egyptian novelist Alaa Al Aswany explains how a nation rediscovered itself by rising up against dictatorship

Alaa Al Aswany is the author of the acclaimed *The Yacoubian Building* and other best-selling works of fiction. He is also a longtime political columnist for independent Egyptian newspapers and one of the founding members of the political movement against the Mubarak regime known as *Kifaya* (Enough). His new book of nonfiction is *On the State of Egypt: What Made the Revolution Inevitable*. *Cairo Review* Managing Editor Scott MacLeod interviewed Al Aswany in Cairo on February 16, 2011.

CAIRO REVIEW: *In* The Yacoubian Building *and* Chicago, *despite the Egyptian decay and misery you portrayed, your characters contain a spark of hope.*
ALAA AL ASWANY: I was always optimistic, I was accused of being too optimistic by some friends. I believed that at some point there would be a revolution in Egypt. I said that in many interviews, including with the *New York Times* in 2008. I tried to understand the Egyptian people as a novelist. I read carefully the history of this country. The 1919 revolution was not expected. The British embassy [thought] that the Egyptians weren't going to react to the decision to send Saad Zaghloul into exile, but all of a sudden there was a revolution. Any country at some point is already in a revolutionary state, waiting for a stimulus to make the revolution. That is exactly what happened on January 25. Forty thousand bloggers called for the manifestations. It came at the right time. The whole of Egypt was waiting for any stimulus, and they gave the stimulus.

CAIRO REVIEW: *Why now?*
ALAA AL ASWANY: There is a critical moment. Egyptians could tolerate poverty. You can live with poverty as far as you think it's fair, as far as you think it's going to improve if you work hard. But what is intolerable is the injustice, when you believe what is happening is not fair and there is no hope for the future. I believe that at some

point you become really prepared to revolt. Why this revolution? First, because of the masses. We're talking about twelve to fifteen million people. And second, the demand was not a local or professional demand. They were demanding the end of the whole system.

CAIRO REVIEW: *Authoritarian regimes from Iraq to Egypt to Morocco to Libya have been so durable, and you've had injustice for so many years.*
ALAA AL ASWANY: One deep lesson of what happened in Egypt is that we don't need an American invasion to get rid of a dictator. We can do it ourselves without all the casualties or occupying another country. And we did that in eighteen days. This is the end of an era of the post-independence dictatorships, which were the model for the region. It's a matter of time for the other dictators. I could give an exception for the Gulf countries because they have enough money to make their people satisfied or to delay the revolution.

CAIRO REVIEW: *After thirty years of the Mubarak regime in Egypt, were there specific factors that helped reach this point?*
ALAA AL ASWANY: The situation in the last ten years. I was against this regime from the very beginning. When I wrote during the 1990s, there were people defending the regime. They were saying, 'Look, [President Mubarak] is doing his best." But during the last ten years, it became impossible to defend the regime. You have a person who is over eighty years old who is still in power and he doesn't feel that this is a strange situation. Also, it was really unacceptable to Egyptians that during the last ten years he started to push his son [Gamal Mubarak as a potential successor]. This was very insulting to Egyptians, that they are going to be inherited as if we were chickens. Egyptians are very proud. We felt in the last ten years there was a real deterioration of the value of Egypt, inside and outside. And, the police brutality has become unbelievable. It's not only for political purposes. Khaled Said [a young Egyptian killed in police custody in Alexandria in 2010] was a very good example. Egyptians are forced to go to work in the Gulf countries, many times in inhuman conditions, and you have no government to look out for you.

CAIRO REVIEW: *Were there recent sparks?*
ALAA AL ASWANY: Of course, the Khaled Said story was very, very, very significant. The people became angry, like never before. Second, there is network of organizations that was not present during the 1990s. We were lacking the network that could organize all the people together and we could [announce] the schedule of the revolution. This happened through Facebook. The Khaled Said Facebook group reached

four hundred and fifty thousand people. [The parliamentary elections] were unbearable. They didn't bother to hide what they were doing. They are telling you as an Egyptian, you are nothing.

CAIRO REVIEW: *Would the revolution have happened if it hadn't happened in Tunisia with the ouster of President Ben Ali?*
ALAA AL ASWANY: Yes. The Tunisia revolution accelerated the Egyptian revolution. It gave you a model and showed to you, yes, it is possible. But the objective reasons for a revolution were present. We began to call for the change of the regime in 2003, so I think it would have happened anyway. But we were inspired by the Tunisians.

CAIRO REVIEW: *Where were you on January 25?*
ALAA AL ASWANY: I knew from the very beginning it was going to be a revolution, from the moment I saw the manifestations. I have a Spanish friend, a journalist who covered the Eastern Europe revolutions. He told me that if you can move these masses—and I could see in their faces how determined they were—the fall of this regime is a matter of time. That day, I knew there would be a manifestation, but I didn't expect it to be the revolution.

CAIRO REVIEW: *When did you realize what it was?*
ALAA AL ASWANY: I participated in many demonstrations. So I said fine, I will finish my work on my novel and then after finishing this chapter I will eat and then I will go to salute my friends. I was expecting four hundred people in front of the syndicate of journalists—I know all of them—with ten thousand soldiers. But when I saw them, I realized there was a historic moment, that it was very different. I joined the revolution on January 25 at 5 p.m. I had once written that if we have five hundred thousand protesters in Cairo, the regime will fall. I found myself with one million people.

CAIRO REVIEW: *There were hard times after January 25.*
ALAA AL ASWANY: Yes, eighteen days. In the first speech of Mubarak, he tried to blackmail the Egyptians emotionally, saying "I defended this land and I will die [in this country]." There were many parents and many other people who became really confused. At 2 a.m. I talked for about thirty minutes [in Tahrir Square], trying to explain to people that we are asking for our rights. We are not acting impolitely with anybody. What was very helpful to the revolution was that the next day, the regime sent the thugs [into the square] and people were killed. So the influence of the speech was erased in a half hour. You can't say you are the father of Egyptians and at the

same time send thugs. Two people were shot to death next to me on January 28. The next speech, the people were really angry. He was very arrogant, like I don't care about you. People raised their shoes [an Arab gesture of disrespect]. You could see female and male shoes everywhere.

CAIRO REVIEW: *That was the end?*
ALAA AL ASWANY: It was a matter of time. On Friday [February 11], I heard people crying, "He resigned! He resigned!" That was an unbelievable moment. Everybody was dancing. I was very, very happy. I was very happy, and very proud of the people. I felt that I am in a moment where a new Egypt really begins.

CAIRO REVIEW: *But Egypt was left in a bad state after thirty years?*
ALAA AL ASWANY: They are trying to blackmail us by the story of the economic crisis. Fine, for thirty years there was no revolution and there were thirty-five million people living under the line of poverty. This is what they did. What we are going to do is much better. The country has been paralyzed by the dictatorship. People who are efficient rarely get the post. You give the post to the people who are loyal. You don't care if they are efficient or not. They were a bunch of friends of Gamal Mubarak who were the rulers of this country. I think the stolen money is quite enough for a good start for Egypt. We have very efficient people in all domains. If you have a democratic country, a democratic cabinet, and you work hard, we could make out of this country a very strong country in no time.

CAIRO REVIEW: *How will Egypt change?*
ALAA AL ASWANY: I believe that the revolution itself is an achievement. The political results are very important. But the revolution as a human phenomenon is an achievement. The revolution makes much better people. When you participate in it, you regain your ability to say "no." You're not going to accept what you used to take before. You could see the difference between the Egyptians in Tahrir Square from the 25th to the 11th. You see two million people, one third of them are females, and not one single sexual harassment. You have everybody, the rich people and the poor people. The mood was very liberal. When the time of prayer comes, the people who don't pray gave space for the people who pray. On Wednesday when there were thugs attacking us, the Christians protected the people who were praying.

CAIRO REVIEW: *How will Egypt change now?*
ALAA AL ASWANY: Egypt regained its identity. One major consequence of dictatorship is that you lose your identity and you're no [longer] loyal to your country.

And you don't believe that it's really your country and you become frustrated and aggressive and desperate. And I believe that the personality now of Egyptians is very different. I think we regained what we lost in the thirty years. This is going to be very positive.

CAIRO REVIEW: *What are the demands of the revolution?*
ALAA AL ASWANY: Wanting Mubarak out was a very relevant point. The president here is the regime. Now you have remnants of the regime, and they should really be kept away. You must build a new country with new concepts. Even the police are going to be very different after what happened. We will have a new country, a democratic state where the rights are preserved and where you get really what you deserve.

CAIRO REVIEW: *You refer to the remnants. How do you translate the victory in Tahrir to a democratic state?*
ALAA AL ASWANY: I'm talking about the heads. I mean the ministers. These people are dangerous. These people were appointed by Mubarak. They believe in the Mubarak regime. They were absolutely defeated, so I can't really ask them to apply the reforms. That's a joke. And also many of them are accused of corruption and committing crimes. The army made a very good start. By insisting that [they] are not ruling, [they] are not in power politically. [They] are trying to maintain the security inside the country and abroad. During the transition, this is the role of the army and it's very important because if you don't have such a power you could have real troubles during the transition.

CAIRO REVIEW: *How do you ensure that the power of the people is translated into democracy?*
ALAA AL ASWANY: We have our plans. The most important thing is to keep your ability to go to the street. You were able to make manifestations and Mubarak was obliged to step down. This is your real power. If you lose this power, you are going to lose everything. I know personally the leaders of the revolution. There are many. They are confident that at some point they can make the same manifestations, and even more, if they find what has been done [is] not satisfactory to them.

CAIRO REVIEW: *Who are the true leaders of the revolution?*
ALAA AL ASWANY: If you're talking about a kind of historical political leader, we don't have one. But you have leaders of groups and these leaders are very significant. You have the leaders of the workers, the leaders of the bloggers, many people. When they call for manifestations, they know what they are doing.

CAIRO REVIEW: *What role do the old political parties have in Egypt's future?*
ALAA AL ASWANY: Conventional parties like Wafd and Tugamma are very badly viewed because they were manipulated by the government. Other parties are decoration, fabricated by the security state to be used at some point.

CAIRO REVIEW: *What about the Muslim Brotherhood?*
ALAA AL ASWANY: They have acted since they acted in 1928. One of the best results of this revolution is for Western analysts to finally know that the Brotherhood is not really a threat to Egypt. I answered this question at least five thousand times: don't you think if you have democracy the Brotherhood will take over? It's unbelievable. I am very happy I won't have to answer this question anymore. They participated like anyone else but they were not controlling. They are Egyptian citizens and despite the fact that I disagree with their ideas, they have the absolute right to practice their political rights in the democracy. They are mysterious, sometimes they compromise too much, but they are sincere.

CAIRO REVIEW: *What are the revolution's priorities?*
ALAA AL ASWANY: To get the efficient people [into the government] and study the potential of Egypt, which is tremendous. You are going to see the difference. The priority is building a democracy. You must make sure your car is efficient before you think about your destination. We must build a real democratic state and after that I think we will be on the right track. Egypt is going to regain its role.

CAIRO REVIEW: *How do you hold the former regime to account?*
ALAA AL ASWANY: The day before yesterday, you could smell the odor of burning papers all over the state television building. They took out the documents and burned them. There were fights because the employees tried to prevent them from doing it. There is a group of lawyers. They are gathering documents. Money is stolen from the Egyptian people and we are going to bring this money back.

CAIRO REVIEW: *What role have artists played in preparing for this revolution?*
ALAA AL ASWANY: Art by nature is a defense of human values. If you see a movie, or read a novel, then you will find in the core of the art the human values of freedom and equality and justice. You don't create art for nothing. I don't think the art is separated from the revolution. I believe that art is revolutionary by nature. We have the most important generation of writers and filmmakers in the history of Egypt. The revolution makes a sort of renaissance for the whole nation, and artists are no exception. I believe this is going to be a real inspiration. I was inspired. I have many ideas to write about the revolution.

Cairo Review Q&A

Rise of the Brothers

Muslim Brotherhood spokesman Essam El-Erian says that with new political opportunities in post-Mubarak Egypt, the group seeks to "participate, not dominate"

Essam El-Erian is a spokesman and political strategist for the Muslim Brotherhood, founded as a political and social movement in Egypt in 1928. Known for its slogan "Islam is the Solution," the group increasingly speaks the language of democracy and compares itself to Islamist parties in democratic nations like Turkey. El-Erian has spent numerous periods in prison as a leader of a movement formally banned from politics since Egyptian independence in 1952. In 1987 he won a seat in parliament, and in 2005 he helped organize a campaign in which eighty-eight Brotherhood members captured parliamentary seats running as independents. *Cairo Review* Managing Editor Scott MacLeod interviewed El-Erian in Cairo on February 21, 2011.

CAIRO REVIEW: *What happened in Egypt?*
ESSAM EL-ERIAN: A surprise. Till now, it is not yet completed. We are going on the run till now. What's happening is going on, it's still continuing. When the last election [in November and December 2010] was totally rigged, the only place for discussion between the people was the streets. They were pushed out of the parliament. Their representatives were pushed out of the parliament to the street. Then it resulted [in this]. It was delayed one month or one and half months.

CAIRO REVIEW: *Not the first time you had a bad election in Egypt.*
ESSAM EL-ERIAN: But this was a very vulgar one. It was not only the rigging of the election. It was the insulting of the people and the comic scene done by the president himself. He said to the people, "Let them have fun." The people got the lesson and they got to the street "to have fun," enjoy their time. The people were enjoying their time since Tahrir Square.

CAIRO REVIEW: *The Brotherhood has been a banned organization in Egypt.*
ESSAM EL-ERIAN: Outlawed.

CAIRO REVIEW: *Yet you tried to make politics in Egypt anyway.*
ESSAM EL-ERIAN: Not trying. We did politics.

CAIRO REVIEW: *How would you describe the Brotherhood's role in Egypt before January 25?*
ESSAM EL-ERIAN: Before, during and after, the same role: We are working with the people. Our target is the people. Not the power.

CAIRO REVIEW: *But politics is about power.*
ESSAM EL-ERIAN: No, this is your philosophy. This time, now, it is the power of the people, not the power of the regimes.

CAIRO REVIEW: *But what were you doing before January 25, in politics in Egypt as an outlawed organization?*
ESSAM EL-ERIAN: Our structure is the same. Participate, not dominate.

CAIRO REVIEW: *Did you have a party?*
ESSAM EL-ERIAN: What's the role of the party? The role of the party is seeking power, mainly according to the Western theories. But here we are not a party. We are still keeping our mind about our role that we are not only a party. We can practice politics but we are an organization, institution, group working for the people in all aspects of life, not only politics by the narrow perception.

CAIRO REVIEW: *Meaning politics and what else?*
ESSAM EL-ERIAN: Everything, everything you can imagine. We believe in Islam as a way of life: individual, family, societal, social, economical, educational. Everything.

CAIRO REVIEW: *Why do you need an organization for Egyptians to live their lives?*
ESSAM EL-ERIAN: This is duty for all Muslims. It's a duty for all Muslims in the Holy Koran, to advise, to educate, to be with the people. The people need each other. We are with the people, they learn from us and we learn from them.

CAIRO REVIEW: *Why do you need an organization for that if it's not a political party?*
ESSAM EL-ERIAN: But this is our duty also, to organize ourselves. We are not individuals. To keep your Islam, you must be organizing with others.

CAIRO REVIEW: *Did you regret participating in the last election?*
ESSAM EL-ERIAN: Never, never. The prize came on the 25th of January.

CAIRO REVIEW: *Some people urged you to boycott the elections .*
ESSAM EL-ERIAN: Okay, they don't understand.

CAIRO REVIEW: *What was the advantage of the election?*
ESSAM EL-ERIAN: To discover the reality of the regime and to encourage people to be against the regime. There are two ways: to participate according to the state of law, or to be out and the people can determine their fate.

CAIRO REVIEW: *What part did the Brotherhood play on January 25?*
ESSAM EL-ERIAN: Part of the scene, participating in the events, guarding protesters, supplying them by all means they can, organizing them, everything. We are part of the protest.

CAIRO REVIEW: *On a political level?*
ESSAM EL-ERIAN: It's not political. Politics mean parliament, cabinets, this is politics. This is a revolution. It's not politics.

CAIRO REVIEW: *Did you formally call your people, your members, to the streets?*
ESSAM EL-ERIAN: We never call anybody. The people themselves come according to Twitter or Facebook. The masses in the street, they were invited.

CAIRO REVIEW: *So, as an organization you didn't play any role.*
ESSAM EL-ERIAN: You can go back to our statements or announcements, which seemed to be daily. We say only that we are part of this event. We are not leading. We are not organizing. The people organize themselves by themselves, in the square, in the streets, in Alexandria, in Aswan, in Mansoura. The people do everything and we are with them, voice among voices.

CAIRO REVIEW: *Is it only the latest election results that sparked the revolution?*
ESSAM EL-ERIAN: It was the straw that broke the camel's back. It was because of corruption, closing any window for free expression.

CAIRO REVIEW: *What has this revolution achieved?*
ESSAM EL-ERIAN: Changed the people. This is the most important.

CAIRO REVIEW: *How?*
ESSAM EL-ERIAN: Changed the Egyptians. The Egyptians changed themselves and broke the fear inside themselves. They rushed in the streets, and when they discovered

their abilities, discovered their original nature, discovered they can do anything, they can clean the square, clean the streets, organize themselves, sing, dance, pray and dance, they discovered they are Egyptians, Christians, Muslims. There is no split in the society. Muslims and Christians are united. Not according to the regime's "national unity," the [Coptic] pope and sheikh of Al Azhar coming together, no. The ordinary people discovered they are not frightened by Muslims and there is no ghetto for Christians. There is the new discovery of the Egyptian nature.

CAIRO REVIEW: *What else?*
ESSAM EL-ERIAN: Mainly democracy, real Islamic democracy.

CAIRO REVIEW: *You have it now?*
ESSAM EL-ERIAN: No, not yet. This is Egyptian democracy with Islamic flavor, Egyptian flavor. They discover they can make their present and future alone. There is no need for any help from anybody, from any foreign policy. The debate now in the United States is, "Was Bush Junior, or Obama, behind what happened?" You are still thinking that you are mastering the globe. The Egyptians discovered that they—according to their abilities, according to their power—can be independent. So, it's not only democracy, it's independence. This is a new independence for the Egyptians. I hope that America can discover also itself, that is not the overwhelming sovereignty in the whole world. It's not the Allah, the God, for the world. That it can live beside others. We are not of course as strong as America, economically, militarily, but the power of the people is the same.

CAIRO REVIEW: *What else has the revolution achieved, since it's not finished?*
ESSAM EL-ERIAN: The president stepped down. His men are still in power, they must step down also. A new cabinet must come, a new parliament, a new president, a civilian one. This transfer of power to civilians is very important. They discover that the army can be a guard, not a political army. It will take time, maybe five years to bring a democratic system and to train the people to vote. Trial and error. It can take time, but we are on the right path and this is very important.

CAIRO REVIEW: *What are the next steps?*
ESSAM EL-ERIAN: The next step is transfer of power, of course.

CAIRO REVIEW: *How will this happen?*
ESSAM EL-ERIAN: Look, sir, surely you studied the history of revolutions in France, in America. I think you had some time from George Washington until the constitution. How long? Ten years? Twenty years? We need time.

CAIRO REVIEW: *What's the next step?*
ESSAM EL-ERIAN: I don't know. There is still debate between the military, cabinet, the media, the intelligence and the people. The debate is still going on.

CAIRO REVIEW: *What does the Brotherhood see as the best solution for going forward now?*
ESSAM EL-ERIAN: Cleaning the country, by the political meaning, because [officials of the former regime] are corrupt . They need to be brought to justice, the stolen wealth needs to be restored, the people who are still in power from the last regime must be out, and this needs of course pressure. The people are ready. They are still not indoors. They are ready to be pouring to the streets again if there is no meeting with their demands.

CAIRO REVIEW: *So you want them all [from the regime] to be arrested?*
ESSAM EL-ERIAN: Of course, it can be step by step. But people want to see something. The media are still controlled by those people, all the media. No changes till now.

CAIRO REVIEW: *Is there active resistance on the part of the regime?*
ESSAM EL-ERIAN: Is this history or is this investigation? You are asking as a prosecutor. If an American comes to interview us as Muslim Brotherhood, he knocks at the door and we say yes or no. America is doing fatal mistakes as America, and you know what I mean. It must review its strategy and listen to the people, not listen to the regimes. You are biased till now, biased. You are hypocritical. This is not beneficial for America. The people here need to listen to American people not American administration. Please, that's enough. People here said enough to Mubarak and they are ready to say enough for everybody. That's enough.

CAIRO REVIEW: *Are you saying that America is interfering in this revolution now?*
ESSAM EL-ERIAN: Of course, it was a fatal mistake to be hesitating from the start, and till now they are hesitating. They don't get the message till now.

CAIRO REVIEW: *Is America against the revolution?*
ESSAM EL-ERIAN: Look, it's an international game. It was between intelligence and government and military. Now the people are in the game. There is no leadership to negotiate with, to satisfy them by anything. It is demands of the people. This is a revolution. Now the people need to have democracy, a real democracy. And democracy is not an American invention or French invention, it's a humanitarian principle. Islam is compatible with democracy. You are still in your country, in your media, literature, in your news, still speaking the same old language. This will create catastrophic consequences

for the whole region. Why are you silent about what's happening in Libya now, a massacre in Libya now. Your new friend Gadhafi is killing people in the streets. Bush junior said that, "We committed a fatal mistake when we supported dictatorships for sixty years," but you came back to the previous support. Why? It's time now to discover that Israel is not the only democratic oasis in the region. We can have many democratic oases. Can you deal with all as the same? This is an historical moment. I hope you can review yourselves. It's not advice. I'm a very little man in a very little organization in a little country and you are mastering the globe. But it's time to discover realities, not to run the same way, to go the same way. And we can be friends, the people of America, people of Egypt, Arab people, Muslims. You know, there is the fall of the legend of Al-Qaeda. The legend of 11 September also has fallen. There is the fall of false theories about terrorism, about Islam, about many things. This is a moment of truth. I hope we can discover ourselves, all of us.

CAIRO REVIEW: *Is the Brotherhood creating a political party now?*
ESSAM EL-ERIAN: We are ready. We are not going to run in the presidential elections with a candidate. We are not targeting to have a majority in the coming parliament. We are not speaking on behalf of the people. Our demands are the same demands of the people. We don't have a special agenda. We are not going to negotiate anything for our own interests. Our prisoners still in jail. We are not looking to bring them out alone. All detainees must come together. We are not going to have party for ourselves alone. All Egyptians are to have the same rights. We are not to dominate. We are going to participate. All of this is not to send message, it's our policy. We do it and we believe in it.

CAIRO REVIEW: *Are you suggesting that if you fielded candidates in all constituencies, you could win a majority?*
ESSAM EL-ERIAN: We are not targeting such thing.

CAIRO REVIEW: *Why not run candidates everywhere?*
ESSAM EL-ERIAN: This is not our strategy. Why not? It's up to us, not to others.

CAIRO REVIEW: *What's the reason?*
ESSAM EL-ERIAN: I told you from the start, we are not just a political party. We are not seeking power. I say that frankly. Believe us.

CAIRO REVIEW: *What's your program?*
ESSAM EL-ERIAN: We said to them all, wait and see, wait and see. Our program will be in the proper time.

CAIRO REVIEW: *Will it endorse a civil state?*
ESSAM EL-ERIAN: Of course. Islam never talked about a religious state. Islam from the start is pro-civil state, in which the nation is the source of power, the nation elects the president, elects the parliament. Accountability, transparency and multiplicity. This is a civil state.

CAIRO REVIEW: *Why did the Brotherhood propose an* ulema *council for this civil state?*
ESSAM EL-ERIAN: We in that debate said that this council is cancelled. It was a wrong idea, written in a wrong language.

CAIRO REVIEW: *What about disallowing a woman, or a Christian, to be president?*
ESSAM EL-ERIAN: Everything can be reviewed. It's one interpretation of many interpretations.

CAIRO REVIEW: *You agree that this will be an important signal if this remains in your Brotherhood program.*
ESSAM EL-ERIAN: The election of president is not our opinion only. It's the rule of the people. If the people elect women, if the people elect Christian, it's up to them. We cannot stop this.

CAIRO REVIEW: *Why not be in favor of it?*
ESSAM EL-ERIAN: We are not going to have a candidate, neither men, neither Muslim, neither women. We are not going to have a candidate now, at all.

Cairo Review Q&A

A More Assertive Arab Foreign Policy

Former Ambassador to the United States Nabil Fahmy believes that a democratic Egypt will not abandon its strategic commitment to peace but will pursue a more pro-active approach in international relations

Nabil Fahmy is the dean of the School of Global Affairs and Public Policy at the American University in Cairo. A career diplomat, he served as Egypt's ambassador to the United States from 1999–2008, and as ambassador to Japan between 1997 and 1999. He has also been a member of Egypt's mission to the United Nations in New York as well as a senior government advisor on nuclear disarmament. After Egypt's revolution began on January 25, he became a member of the informal group of "wise men" who met with government officials and demonstrators. *Cairo Review* Managing Editor Scott MacLeod interviewed Fahmy in Cairo on February 22, 2011.

CAIRO REVIEW: *How did you get involved as one of the "wise men"?*
NABIL FAHMY: January 25 was a holiday, Police Day. I live close to Tahrir Square and was very curious to see whether the announced demonstration was going to actually develop. It turned out to be even larger than expected even by the youth organizers of the event. So that was sort of the first surprise. The large presence of the police also tended to heighten the tension on both sides. This was a very strange beginning.

CAIRO REVIEW: *What did you encounter?*
NABIL FAHMY: Against all odds, it remained peaceful from the side of the demonstrators. Whether they were faced by violence or not, they did not take the initiative of using violence. They only defended themselves in certain circumstances. To have this size of a demonstration is not normal for Cairo. You normally have economic and social topics being the genesis of the demonstrations of much smaller size. I have young children and the youth were the voice behind the protests, so as a father I had an eye on what is happening here. That was really my first reckoning of how serious these kids were.

CAIRO REVIEW: *What happened?*
NABIL FAHMY: My son came in with eight or nine of his friends who were demonstrating after the curfew was announced. They came to have a meal. Because I was a father, I said, "Okay, why don't you all sleep over." They said, "Why?" I said, "Because there is a curfew." They said, "Who decides there's a curfew? We own the country." That kind of statement could be taken as naïve. For me, it was an indication that they wanted to own the country. This was a commitment they were making. It wasn't a passing comment that was made rhetorically. Within an hour, they were all back on the street demonstrating again. Was a societal change being made here, led by the youth? That was really the beginning of my personal involvement in it. I wanted to see how this was going, and to make sure that rational minds remained the ultimate deciding factor. I also felt that these kids actually needed to find fulfillment and satisfaction in their aspirations. Otherwise we were going to have a generation that was going to be tremendously disappointed.

CAIRO REVIEW: *That was a personal turning point?*
NABIL FAHMY: The second turning point, on a personal level, was the day when the hooligans went into Tahrir Square on horses and camels and had a pitched battle that was broadcast on television. Watching peaceful demonstrators battle hooligans for twelve hours with no one intervening, for me, was just simply a shock. At that point, I thought, "How could we, as a generation with this set of values, hand over a country to the younger generation?" That's really the moment I decided that I cannot remain just a passive supporter of the objectives of the demonstrators.

CAIRO REVIEW: *So how did you become involved with the "wise men"?*
NABIL FAHMY: On that same day, coincidentally, a group of independent public figures, from different walks of life, some lawyers, some engineers, architects, former diplomats, and businessmen, released a statement that essentially called for the president to hand over power to his vice president. He could remain in office as a titular president for the remainder of his tenure, provided that he handed over power, and a number of other steps were taken: dissolving the parliament and Shura Council, establishing a transitional committee for changing the government, changing the leadership of the majority party, ending the state of emergency. So they set forward a seven-point plan, to start the process of ending the Mubarak rule in a dignified fashion. Not only ending it, but beginning the rebuilding of Egypt constitutionally, legally and politically. That evening, I contacted them and said I had been informed of the statement and, if they wanted my support, I would join. They did, and consequently a group of about twelve was established and became the signatories of what

others called the "Wise Men Group." It was an informal, independent group. No one had any party affiliations of whatever sort, in the former majority party or any of the minority parties. We were not all men, in spite of the name. There were women in the group.

CAIRO REVIEW: *What did the group's work entail?*
NABIL FAHMY: The group mandated two of our members to go and meet the vice president [Omar Suleiman], and convey to him the proposals. He listened attentively, but his response on the issue of the president mandating authority to the vice president was that this was a non-starter. Then he discussed the other suggestions, regarding the parliament and constitution, and said he would look into those, although he did get into an explanation of why these things could not happen quickly. We then went to meet the prime minister [Ahmed Shafiq], who basically said the same thing. After that, we were very careful to continue to support the demonstrators, and to continue to look for solutions. We were not trying to find a compromise between the two sides. We were trying to actually help build the new Egypt, but do it in a fashion where the demonstrators came out with results rather than simply lost.

CAIRO REVIEW: *What was the group's relationship with the protesters?*
NABIL FAHMY: We started to meet with the representatives of the demonstrators. They had many representatives, but nobody really mandated to speak on their behalf. There were at least five different groups. They all came speaking for their own group and it was interesting because you had the groups like the Muslim Brotherhood youth, not the elders, but the youth movement, which are of course religious in inclination, and secularists also there.

CAIRO REVIEW: *What did they tell you?*
NABIL FAHMY: They were unified in their demands for what had to happen now, and committed to working together, in spite of their different opinions about how to build Egypt in the future. They said that openly: "No, we don't necessarily agree on what Egypt should look like, but what is required now is the president leaves, and then [implement] all of the other six points that we had made." They asked us to convey these opinions to the government, but not to negotiate on their behalf, which was fine with us. Since they weren't mandated, we didn't feel comfortable getting a mandate from those who were not mandated. These were extremely insightful and enlightening to us, youth from different walks of life. Some were affluent, some were less affluent. The majority was from Egyptian public universities. Some had gone to university abroad, but not that many. They were all extremely well educated politically, and they

knew exactly what they wanted. They wanted a new system, they wanted a new way of governance, and then they had specific targets in the short term. For example, the president had to leave. Then you would address all the constitutional and legal issues, but without the top target, they would not move. Our approach was a bit different, in terms of the first target, but they at least respected our integrity, and believed we would convey their message as told to us.

CAIRO REVIEW: *What happened next?*
NABIL FAHMY: At the same time, the vice president was meeting with a larger group of opposition leaders that he chose. It did not include anyone from our group, except businessmen. So there were many different processes going on here. What was very amusing and interesting was that the vice president was essentially meeting the "political parties plus" but the political parties had no influence whatsoever in Tahrir Square, in the demonstrations. He should have been meeting "demonstrators plus some of the parties," rather than meeting the parties plus some of the demonstrators. That in many ways reflected the lack of sensitivity to what had actually happened. One of the demonstrators we had met at the end of our meetings had mentioned, "Oh, the vice president is meeting opposition leaders from the parties and people he has chosen. They are trying to control the agenda. We will."

CAIRO REVIEW: *And they did?*
NABIL FAHMY: And they did. They increased the pressure in different parts of Egypt systematically in the next few days. In all candor, they were strengthened and supported by mishandling on the government side at every point in time. If you look at the sequence of the president's speeches, substance-wise he actually gave quite a lot even before he resigned. But it was done piecemeal, always late, and always in a form that made it very difficult to accept, and very easy for those who did not want to accept it to say, "You shouldn't believe this." As I mentioned, [the regime] rejected our proposal for the president to hand over power to the vice president. He finally announced he would accept that proposal fourteen days later, the day before he resigned. At that point, you couldn't even convey that to the other side. It was dead on delivery at that point.

CAIRO REVIEW: *Is there anything President Mubarak could have done?*
NABIL FAHMY: There is the issue of when the President announced that he would not run for office again and that he would not leave Egypt, he wanted to die in Egypt. Egyptians are emotional. Egyptian society was actually divided on this, not the demonstrators, but the society. Many people said, "Well, this is a respectful way out. Why don't we accept?" President Mubarak for his first ten to fifteen years had a very

good record as president. Most of the criticisms and arguments came in the second half of his tenure. The president made the speech at night. The next day, by about two o'clock, you had the hooligans going into Tahrir Square with the camels and horses. To have the violence go on for twelve hours on live television. It turned the most passive Egyptian against the system and in support of the demonstrators. That killed the president's offer that he would not run again and he wanted to die in Egypt. That killed all of the emotional support that he could have gotten from the public. It was those supporters of the majority party that organized, financed, and encouraged the hooligans to go in to Tahrir Square, and those that remained passive allowing these battles to go on for twleve hours, who turned the tide in terms of the political support of society for the demonstrators. There was no return from there on. There simply was no return.

CAIRO REVIEW: *Where did that put the wise men group?*
NABIL FAHMY: We went down to Tahrir Square the day afterwards. It took us forty-five minutes to cross the square because of the crowds and we received a tremendously warm welcome, but very loud chants: "He leaves! He leaves! He leaves! He leaves!" One was touched by this. On the one hand, they were open to dialogue with people who were looking for a way out and not necessarily completely responsive in the short term to their emotional desires. They welcomed us very well, but they were sending us a strong message: "He leaves." None of us going into the square that day, after the violence, was ready to ask for less.

CAIRO REVIEW: *That was a turning point for Egypt.*
NABIL FAHMY: Another turning point is ironic, but anybody who understands Egypt should recognize this. The minute the army went down in the streets, the government lost control. Let me rephrase that: the minute the army hit the street, it was clear that the demonstrators had won, because the Egyptian army does not shoot at Egyptian civilians. It has never done it, and its code of honor is that it will not. They are now between you and the people. If the choice is put to them, "You have to make a choice," they've already announced that they will go with the people. That's always been their position, so rather than be a source of stability and strength for the government, it actually was a source of stability and strength for the demonstrators. So you had the army, and the chant of "we and the army are one" from the demonstrators. This was confirmed in all the public statements from the army. There was not a single reference to the president in the first statement, not a single reference to the government. It was always the army and the people and that's a continuous message. Then the army issued a statement, "We as an army high commission have met and we are

in constant session." For analysts of army statements, that means, "We are watching. We are no longer a passive participant here. We are watching as an active participant." In that same statement, they say, "We support the legitimate demands of the demonstrators." So you see a political shift here. The first mistake was sending the army down, but [the regime] had to do that because of what happened with the police. But that actually strengthened the demonstrators. Towards the end, when it became closer to the army being asked, "Well, you're going to have to use force," they knew they would not. But they did not want to disobey an order. So they issued a statement saying, "Okay, we are watching, and we will make our own decisions."

CAIRO REVIEW: *So the army role was decisive here?*
NABIL FAHMY: You had in the last twenty-four hours an expectation of a statement from the president. But it didn't come out as "I will mandate Omar Suleiman"–which is what we had suggested much earlier—and the army saying "We will guarantee that he does that." Instead, you had the army waiting to watch the people in the street, and when the people in the streets said, "No," the army said, "Enough is enough."

CAIRO REVIEW: *What lessons do you see in your efforts?*
NABIL FAHMY: You can draw three conclusions from this. One, it's a wonderful case study in how not to manage a crisis. I mean, all of the elements of what not to do were exercised. Second, it clearly showed that there was this huge gap between what the presidency thought was reality and what was the reality on the ground. That's a function of long-term government and age and isolation. Thirdly, it shows you the true limitations of power. In other words, the tank on the street was less effective than mobile phones and Facebook. The tank was there but it couldn't be used, they couldn't shoot. It is a testimony to what constitutes power in this day and age. Military power is, and will continue to be, important. But the power of communication, the power to network, the power to organize—because we live in a transparent world and you can't simply react without ramifications worldwide—is extremely important to take into account here.

CAIRO REVIEW: *And, as you said, the Egyptian youth showed a great deal of political maturity.*
NABIL FAHMY: How did they have such clarity of thought? I remember once in our discussions, just to understand the limits of how far we could go, I asked one of them a couple of questions. He responded "We have just undertaken revolution. This is not about technicalities. It is about a revolution, and you all should understand this. We want to change the system. Help us develop the mechanics to change the system, but nothing less than changing the system will serve us." We talked about everything

from constitutional reform to the reconciliation process, and so on, and one of them shot back—they shot back in their emotion, but not once did they lose tempers, did they speak impolitely or inappropriately, these were truly admirable kids—one shot back and said, "Gentlemen, my friend was standing right here at my shoulder when he was killed. So don't get lost. This has to be commensurate with the loss that I have and that his family has." It was actually quite touching.

CAIRO REVIEW: *You have faith?*
NABIL FAHMY: Egyptians are retaking ownership of their own country. Now, that will have implications. If you engage them in building the politics and legal system of the new Egypt, you will have progress. If you don't, you are going to have problems, because they will not back off.

CAIRO REVIEW: *The challenges ahead?*
NABIL FAHMY: The military has been exceptionally astute politically from day one, to my astonishment. How subtle they've been, and how careful they have been. Now that they are also the governors of the country, the leaders of the country, they are going to have to satisfy the political leanings of everyone, and that's a much more complicated situation. They, on the one hand, have announced a program to hand over in six months civilian rule and hold four elections—three elections and a referendum. They need to be continuously transparent and they need to be continuously inclusive because this is not about changing the president, it's about changing Egypt.

CAIRO REVIEW: *Why do you think the revolution came now?*
NABIL FAHMY: We were going toward a political confrontation in the summer of 2011 because we would have an election for president in the fall. There was a big question whether President Mubarak was going to run again, or nominate his son, and who else, so there were a lot of questions here about that. Add to that that we have a population where 56 percent is younger than twenty-five years old, an anxious population, an impatient population, a vigorous population, looking for their own future, trying to determine their own future. One had to expect that we were going to reach a boil at one point. Did I expect a revolution? No. But, yes, I expected political tension. Why did it reach the point that it did? The first thing is that the demographic mix is ripe for that. Secondly, there was this blatantly arrogant result in the last parliamentary elections in November where the majority party got 97 percent of the seats. You have to be a political amateur to even want to achieve that kind of majority, because it means putting all of the opposition outside of parliament against you, even though they differ from each other.

CAIRO REVIEW: *That was a trigger?*
NABIL FAHMY: So the oil was spilled out there on the street waiting for it to be lit up. It was lit up by Tunis. What lit it up in January rather than June was basically the events in Tunis. Had it happened differently, it could have possibly have led to a compromise of the president not running for office again and without everybody being thrown out of government.

CAIRO REVIEW: *As an Egyptian diplomat, how do you see the international dimension to the political change in Egypt?*
NABIL FAHMY: I've always criticized fundamentalists because they don't think rationally about certain things. But on foreign interference, I'm a fundamentalist. I simply do not encourage foreign players to get engaged as long as violence is not used against civilians. The reason is not because I have a problem with the moral issues, quite the contrary. I understand people raising questions about violence and human rights and all that. And expressions about violations of human rights are completely understandable as long as the facts are there. It's just because all countries have their own challenges, they have their own political calendars, and their own interests, their own priorities. And they may not be consistent with ours. I don't like to determine, define, or even calibrate my own domestic agenda with a domestic agenda that is foreign.

CAIRO REVIEW: *How do you evaluate the U.S. posture during the days in Tahrir Square?*
NABIL FAHMY: Initially, it was clear they were lost and completely surprised. Lost, they should not have been. Surprised, I can understand, because we all were, but only on timing. For years, the U.S. body politic has had no respect for Arab public opinion. When we would convey the public sentiment to our American interlocutors they would ignore or snicker! I am sure this will stop now. Nevertheless, I think President Obama's last comments about being inspired by the youth touched the square tremendously. When Obama said, "I was inspired by these kids," they felt they were heard. Everything in between that, they frankly were not focused on.

CAIRO REVIEW: *Could the U.S. have done anything differently to better influence events?*
NABIL FAHMY: I did not want them to influence events. Even if we failed, this had to be an Egyptian thing. I didn't want it to be tarnished by a foreign element. But let me add to that. Frankly, sending [former U.S. ambassador to Egypt] Frank Wisner was a big mistake. I understand why America would feel obliged to do that. But, in

fact, it was over by then. It again reflected to you that they did not understand what was happening in the street. The minute the army went into the street, the demonstrators won. At the end of the day, President Mubarak was leaving, one way or the other, the minute the army went into the street. So sending the emissary here, and then you had contradicting reports about what he actually said, and then conflicting reports about Frank's opinion and the administration's opinion, that was frankly a weak point. I'm not criticizing Frank himself, I'm simply saying that was the weakest point of the process. I know that they have been constantly in touch with the presidency and the military and with anyone that they could get in touch with here to keep emphasizing to them, "don't use force." Generally speaking, President Obama's statements were much better than any European statements where he focused on Egypt's demonstration and Egypt's rights, whereas some of the European statements immediately jumped into "You have to respect your agreements with Israel." They brought in the Israeli debate even though this was a purely Egyptian thing.

CAIRO REVIEW: *We didn't see anti-American or anti-Israel messages in Tahrir.*
NABIL FAHMY: It's an interesting point that in all of my discussions with everybody here, foreign policy was not mentioned once by the demonstrators, not once. They didn't argue about it, they didn't reject it, they didn't send any messages to anybody. When the army took charge, the army said that they would respect international agreements, just to calm people's nerves. After the demonstrations ended, the demonstrators said that they were changing Egypt domestically and that they would respect international agreements and discuss these later. So this was not about foreign policy. What's important now, frankly, is to build a better Egypt. We will need some time.

CAIRO REVIEW: *Will the revolution reorient Egypt as a more nationalist society with a more nationalist foreign policy?*
NABIL FAHMY: The people have taken charge of the government. They are going to hold their government officials more accountable in the short term. In all of our actions, including foreign policy, while we will have strategic agendas, they are much more sensitive to urgent tactical concerns and pressures. I'll give you an example. I don't see the situation on the borders in Gaza—I never did and I still don't see—being a tenable situation. That's not that I support Hamas, or that the revolution supports Hamas. But we need to find a creative way to ensure that the border breathes and preserves security at the same time. It is not viable politically to say, "They have done wrong, therefore we will apply a blockade." Yes, you will see a much stronger Egypt in responding to double standards, in responding to, for example, Israel's settlement policy, and in emphasizing the interests of developing countries in the World Trade

Organization. These kids, this youth, and this society have taken charge now and they want to be engaged and they are holding public officials accountable.

CAIRO REVIEW: *So that is bound to affect Egypt's foreign policy posture on some issues?*
NABIL FAHMY: If we do it right, we will be under the same pressures that everybody is under in a democratic country. Where, yes, we have strategic goals and you need to find a balance with your people of what you can do in the short term and what you can do in the long term. But you can't ignore short-term concerns. [American officials] would come very often to me when I was in Washington and say, "Oh, we can't do that, we have congressional elections." Well, now *we'll* have them, too. So, you can stop giving me that, or you're going to start hearing it from me at the same time. When we would say, "The Israelis need to go back to the 1967 borders," [American officials] would say, "Well, the Israelis have a coalition government, and there is this small, minute, political party that is way off the wall here but holds the seat in some subcommittee." Well, we have it too. So yes, you are going to see a much more assertive Egypt, an Egypt that is not less concerned with strategic objectives—they won't change—but much more concerned with immediate short-term things. That's good, if you go back through the history of the Middle East. Egypt always led the region by being the trendsetter in ideas, in political, economic, and social trends. That's where we are going to be now again. We may not be raising the flag of pan-Arabism, but we will be raising the flag of a stronger, more proactive, better Arab world. We won't fall back in history, but we will go forward. Frankly, I have been annoyed by this for a number of years, and I said it when I was in service: we have to be less reactive and more proactive. When you are reactive, especially for a medium-sized country in a global society, there are so many things everywhere in the world you get dizzy reacting to all of these things. You have to, especially in your region, be one of the forces that determine the agenda. We will be a more useful, more valuable [partner] to the U.S. than ever before, because we will have more influence in the region than ever before. Will we dance to your music all the time? We actually never did.

CAIRO REVIEW: *So Washington has to get used to a different Egypt?*
NABIL FAHMY: I think it's a different region. If you [Americans] look at it only from the perspective of the Arab–Israeli conflict, you will lose. With the Arab–Israeli conflict, frankly, you have not been particularly effective in pushing it forward. Look at the region differently. It's not the same region that can swallow anything as long as you keep looking at the longer perspective. Whether it's those in government dealing with government, or the analysts writing about what's happening in Egypt from Massachusetts Avenue, they don't understand what's actually happening in Egypt.

CAIRO REVIEW: *How will the revolution affect Israel and the Egyptian–Israeli peace treaty?*
NABIL FAHMY: This revolution actually serves Israel as well. It may not serve the Israeli right. It definitely will not serve those who do not want peace between Israel and the Arab world, those who do not want a two-state solution. They will hear our voice much louder when they hear the Arab voice. It will be much louder when they enter east Jerusalem and try to place Jewish settlers in that part of town. Therefore, the Israeli public will realize how wrong these steps are from the Israeli right and how this will lead to postponing peace. Yes, it may worry people initially, but I think it will energize the peace movements on both sides, give a strong message to the right that if you go too far, your own people will push you out, not us.

CAIRO REVIEW: *How will the new Egypt affect the Arab world?*
NABIL FAHMY: Parts of the Arab world will worry, because once again they will see us ahead of the curve. But more and more, we will try to take them with us, rather than try to do it alone. If we do this properly and if [political change] slowly seeps into their systems, then they can actually do this without the confrontations that we had to go through.

CAIRO REVIEW: *Considering that Islamist groups antagonistic to Israel may be in the government for the first time, what is the risk to the Egyptian–Israeli peace treaty?*
NABIL FAHMY: The Islamist movement had a role without having any responsibility in the past. They were in parliament, in the press, but they didn't have the responsibility of governing. They have both won and lost from this process. What will determine their weight, is, will the secularists continue to be activists, continue to be engaged, continue to turn this energy into political action plans and parties? That's what will determine the Muslim Brotherhood's role. The Muslim Brotherhood was not the leader of these demonstrations, but they were there, and they were significantly there. How would this influence the effect on U.S. relations or relations with Israel and the Israeli peace agreement? The only statement mentioned throughout this process was made by some spokesperson from the Brotherhood. He said Egypt would respect all of its agreements both internationally and regionally, but review them at the same time. I don't see anything wrong with that position. The Muslim Brotherhood has always made their position clear. Their agenda is mostly domestic, it's not based on foreign policy. If I was a foreigner watching from abroad, I would be applauding that somehow, something got all of the Egyptian middle class and the secularists to come out and be activists. So I'm not following things with too much anxiety.

Cairo Review Q&A

FROM DICTATORSHIP TO DEMOCRACY

Political analyst Amr Hamzawy says that Egypt's new challenge is to transform the "protesting citizen" into a "participating citizen"

Amr Hamzawy is research director and a senior associate at the Carnegie Middle East Center in Beirut, and a political science professor at Cairo University. He also serves on the Middle East Advisory Council of Human Rights Watch. He is the author of the recent books *Between Religion and Politics* and *The Arab Future: Contemporary Debates on Democracy, Political Islam, and Resistance*. *Cairo Review* Managing Editor Scott MacLeod interviewed Hamzawy in Cairo on February 19, 2011.

CAIRO REVIEW: *What does the revolution mean for Egypt?*
AMR HAMZAWY: Let's start chronologically, with the significance of January 25. I guess the major, major point of January 25 was that citizens for the first time regained the street as a political arena. [This] entailed the fact that the barrier of fear was [made relative], at least to the extent that citizens could express themselves freely, they were able to express themselves in big numbers freely, and to try to stand their ground in front of brutal security apparatus. The numbers which took out to the street in Cairo, Alexandria, and elsewhere were not the numbers which we expected. No one expected it to turn that way. Everyone was expecting to see the same familiar faces of [the Egyptian opposition group] *Kifaya* and a couple of activists who we have been following in the last years. January 28 was the real beginning of the citizen's revolution in Egypt in different ways. We did not only have young members of protest networks and movements, we had cross-cutting representation of different social groups, highly representative. We had a massive increase in the numbers of demonstrators and we had an increase in the nationwide nature of what was going on. The last time Egyptians took to the streets in similar numbers was 1919.

CAIRO REVIEW: *The political meaning of that?*
AMR HAMZAWY: Regaining control over the streets meant that people were giving up on whatever they invested hope in, in terms of reforming Egypt and democratizing

Egypt. Some people had invested hope in the reform orientation of the NDP (ruling National Democratic Party), others invested hope in opposition parties and movements, be it the Wafd or the Ikhwan (Muslim Brotherhood). It was [a testament] to the failure of not only the ruling party but of the opposition parties and movements in pushing reform. It was a constituency of Egyptians coming together in a sustained manner to push democratic demands in a non-ideological manner, in a peaceful manner, and in a clear manner, which really did not need any additional articulation by a leadership. To my mind that was one of the most impressive aspects of the citizens' revolution in Egypt. It was based on a national consensus that emerged in the 'free public space.'

CAIRO REVIEW: *This was surprising?*
AMR HAMZAWY: I was always in favor of doubting how significant 'free public debates' are in Egypt, with whatever 'red lines' we had been having. But it seemed that they had an impact. They created a national consensus where they took that out to the streets, they built on that in articulating their demands. We started with Cairo, Alexandria, and Suez and then in the last days Upper Egyptian governorates coming, like in Minya and Sohag. It developed gradually in terms of sectoral representation, young people, poor segments, middle class, workers, industrial workers, peasants. Finally, we had the urban/rural divide which was transcended in the last days, in the third week. The sheer number who took out to the street to demand Mubarak's resignation was by far more than those who voted for Mubarak in all elections between 1981 and 2005. He never got more than four million, and what we had was definitely more than that.

CAIRO REVIEW: *What were the demands of this national consensus?*
AMR HAMZAWY: The demands of January 25 were at least [Interior Minister Habib] El-Adly's resignation.The demands of January 28 were the removal of the regime. And then around that we moved in a very rational manner between different versions. Well, let him delegate to the vice president. He delegated too late. We are now to the phase of trying to see if we could put Egypt on a safe path towards democratization.

CAIRO REVIEW: *Many were astonished by the events.*
AMR HAMZAWY: The assumption that Egyptians are not willing to challenge authority is based on wrong reading of Egyptian history. Egyptian history has never been a history of submission to rulers. And although no one of us expected it to turn the way it turned, many of us saw the ingredients, with the political backsliding, the socioeconomic crises, and sectarian tensions everywhere, that a change was going to come.

CAIRO REVIEW: *Then what accounts for how the regime was able to maintain such a tight control for thirty years?*
AMR HAMZAWY: The regime went through different phases. The real failure of the regime or the collapse of its legitimacy started in 2005. Up until 2005, Mubarak was not a hated figure. Some people never liked him, some liked him, but the overall performance of Mubarak one could say was more balanced [compared] to [Anwar] Sadat and [Gamal]Abdel Nasser. We had a degree of freedom of expression, a bit of freedom of association. Human rights violations were of course there but they were not as bad as they were under Abdel Nasser. We had more of a market economy, some cases of corruption but not massive-scale corruption. The father-son succession scenario was rumored but was not a reality. But after 2005, Mubarak started to lose track of what was going on in Egypt. He distanced himself from the population, which always appreciated his frankness, his ability to address them and their concerns. Corruption became wide-scale and embedded in the ruling establishment. Gamal Mubarak's succession scenario became a project and was implemented. [There was a] complete backsliding on political freedoms and freedoms of association and expression. [There were] disastrous elections for the Shura Council and People's Assembly. We had growing rates of economic development but they never trickled down. So this was a bleak picture, and add to that the illness of an ailing president who was no longer in charge. The arrogance of the regime reached a point where even an opposition representation in the People's Assembly was no longer tolerated. This pushing out socioeconomically and politically meant ultimately pushing them out to the street.

CAIRO REVIEW: *What was the spark?*
AMR HAMZAWY: Even if you go to the young members of the protest who organized January 25, no one of them expected to see that turnout, no one of them expected to see fifty thousand Egyptians demonstrating. They expected much more modest numbers. So there was an element of surprise, which was definitely related to Tunisia, the discovery by many citizens of Egypt of how weak those authoritarian, autocratic regimes are.

CAIRO REVIEW: *Was there a leader of this revolution?*
AMR HAMZAWY: No. This is something I increasingly find frustrating in our public debate. [People] are trying to substitute the question of institutions and mechanisms with leaders, which is why you are seeing now an increased debate about [Nobel laureate] Ahmed Zewail, and [Arab League Secretary General] Amr Moussa. What is really key as of now is to agree on what is going to happen not only to the constitution but to the political reengineering of Egypt. To open up the system, to create and sustain competitive elections. What will happen in terms of rebuilding and reforming state institutions,

rebuilding the security apparatus, reforming state media. What does it take? The right mix of procedures, mechanisms, institutions, structures, institutional traditions, precedents. This is not being discussed.

CAIRO REVIEW: *Who started the protest on January 25?*
AMR HAMZAWY: There were six groups, which are known, and all of them are now in the January 25 Revolution Youth Coalition, coming from different party affiliations: Al-Ghad (Tomorrow), El-Gabha (Democratic Front), Ikhwan (Brotherhood), and other groups that are liberal or leftist, the April 6 Movement. They coordinated. There was an unorganized segment which in fact starting on January 28 became even more crucial. [Without them] it would have failed. Then the last week, the decisive turning point was the industrial workers and professional associations, the railways, public transportation, basically on strike and [performing] civil disobedience. They were the ones who really pushed the military establishment to force Mubarak to resign.

CAIRO REVIEW: *That was the push?*
AMR HAMZAWY: Right. If he would have delegated ten days after the beginning of the revolution, he would have gotten away with the delegation formula. It was accepted. He always gave too little and too late. This has been Mubarak's recipe in the last five years. Basically, we would have had him as an honorary president and [Vice President] Omar Suleiman would have continued to manage what he was starting to get into: national dialogue, opening up. I was in Tahrir every day. It would have been accepted, to my mind. People would have wished to keep the military establishment out of the direct management of Egyptian politics. After all, we had the 1952 experience, and we had these two years between 1952 and 1954 where democracy was promised and we ended up going in a completely different direction.

CAIRO REVIEW: *What happened on February 10 and 11?*
AMR HAMZAWY: This was a country feeling as if it was going to disintegrate very soon. The army had been out in the streets trying to police a country, but not policing it effectively. The collective psychology by Thursday was expecting only "I resign." What happened was a massive escalation, once again. The march to the [presidential palace] Qasr Al-Oruba, different marches elsewhere, this was really like a country falling apart. So the military had to push him. That's what they did. We don't know much. We know that they gave him the chance to see how the delegation scenario will work out. Since it did not work out, they resorted back to the originally preferred [option] I guess on Thursday, which was for him to step down. And then they pushed him to step down.

CAIRO REVIEW: *How does the youth movement translate the revolution into an actual political system where they have a role?*
AMR HAMZAWY: That's one of the key challenges. Countries which undergo democratic transitions after citizens' revolutions have a very hard time the first years trying to get the right mix of processes, institutions, mechanisms, and safeguards. [These must] ensure the rule of law, the creation of democratic institutions, peaceful competition in the formal political sphere, citizens' participation. Basically, to transfer the protesting and striking citizen from being a protesting and striking citizen into a participating citizen. The key objective is to ensure having fair and competitive parliamentary and presidential elections and safeguarding the competitive and transparent nature of the elections. A whole new set of challenges [is] coming up.

CAIRO REVIEW: *Such as?*
AMR HAMZAWY: How to organize in a meaningful way that gives citizens a chance to participate. One, you go into political parties, you create effective political parties which can claim to represent, which reach out in constituency-building activities, and lobby around platforms and create interest for citizens. Or you depend on civil society. The challenge is key because Egyptians took out to the streets, were out in the streets for three weeks, and now no one knows if they will come back when there are elections. The second challenge: is the constitution, after the amendments, enough to secure peaceful transition to democracy in Egypt? My answer is no. This is a presidential constitution, which gives a president so many prerogatives, does not make him accountable, and would create an autocratic ruler of sorts out of every Egyptian president. I do not believe that presidential systems are best equipped to manage transition periods to democracy. Parliamentary systems are much, much better. This is based on comparative experience. You look at Latin America, Eastern Europe, the Balkans, and Spain, Greece, Portugal. The elected parliament will have to start a new discussion about the constitution and whether we can push successfully to a parliamentary system. A parliamentary system will ensure to my mind higher degrees of citizens' participation in parties and would activate the citizenry of Egypt.

CAIRO REVIEW: *What other challenges do you see?*
AMR HAMZAWY: How to let democracy, as an organizing principle for the Egyptian polity, trickle down to other arenas in society. To really influence each vital sector of society. Be it civil society, education, state institutions, the security apparatus, media, and so on. I mean, how to institutionalize democracy with its key procedures and values not only in formal politics but beyond. The next challenge is, what are you going to do with the military establishment? I mean they are managing Egyptian politics as of now.

But if we are going to build a democratic and civil polity, they will have to be pushed out. Of course, it will be misleading to imagine they will give up and say "you guys do it now." Of course, they would like to retain some role in politics. I'm increasingly convinced that one way to manage it is to go in a similar direction like Turkey and give them a national security council or a similar body, a safeguarding role. In Turkey, they safeguard the republican values. In Egypt, they would have to safeguard democratic values and would have to ensure the civil nature of Egyptian polity, not only against an active role of the military, but also an Islamization of Egyptian politics. I guess they would like to retain that role, but how to devise the mechanism is going to be challenging.

CAIRO REVIEW: *How can you have parliamentary elections when the party system is discredited, you have no or few real political parties?*
AMR HAMZAWY: Existing parties are discredited as part of the autocratic formula of Mubarak. They were domesticated, they fought for minor shares and small gains. They are stagnant and decaying in their structures. They will have to work out a model and strategy to energize and reach out and do some constituency building. There are some active parties as well. Al-Ghad and El-Gabha, of Ayman Nour and Osama Ghazaly Harb, have young members. New parties will be established as well. Just today, the Islamist Al-Wasat party got finally its license. Ultimately, not a single society which transitioned from autocracy to democracy got it right in the first election. Look at what happened in Eastern European countries, you had communists reassembling and coming back.

CAIRO REVIEW: *How strong is the staying power of the remnants of the Mubarak regime?*
AMR HAMZAWY: They were so interwoven with the state institutions, probably one cannot discard the possibility of them reorganizing, reassembling under a new banner. They have the advantage of having representation everywhere in the country. This was a state party and the state party was represented everywhere. I do not expect them to do well in the elections. They will be discredited very soon, once you see the same figures who are well known to Egyptians. I have some good reasons to believe the military establishment does not like them and would really like to do away with that party and its legacy. They might let it participate, reassembled under a new banner, but will not favor it over its competitors.

CAIRO REVIEW: *What is the Muslim Brotherhood's future?*
AMR HAMZAWY: I guess they will have similar troubles like everyone else in the old opposition spectrum. You have real tensions between their young members and

the old guard. They will have to come to a choice if they would like to participate, and establish a political party, they would have to separate institutionally between the *dawa* (religious call) and the political component, which is not easy. This movement has sustained itself since 1928 by being two in one, a social/religious movement and a political arm. Separating will not be easy. On the other hand, they are an organized movement, they have a constituency, and they have a network similar to the NDP, branches which exist everywhere. Probably they will do well, but I do not see them getting a majority. Maybe they will take 20–30 percent if they contest that many seats. Even if they would run candidates for each seat, I don't see them getting a majority.

CAIRO REVIEW: *Is there an unreasonable fear about the Islamization of Egypt, an Islamist takeover?*
AMR HAMZAWY: The 'Islamist takeover' stuff is based on a wrong framing of what happened. It was not an Islamist revolution. There is not a risk of hijacking, but the risk of them being the only organized movement and lobbying democratically to get citizens to join them. If they do it democratically, I cannot say hijacking. They don't command the strategic majority, but if you leave the ground for them, and you do a poor job in organizing, you do not do your homework in terms of constituency building and getting out a convincing platform, then you never know what will happen. Not in the next elections, but in the one after. They are good at constituency building, we know it.

Cairo Review Q&A

SEEKING JUSTICE

Longtime activist Aida Seif El-Dawla demands that Egypt's regime be held accountable for past—and ongoing—human rights abuses

Aida Seif El-Dawla is the cofounder of the El Nadim Center for the Rehabilitation of Victims of Violence and of the Egyptian Association Against Torture. She is also a professor of psychiatry at Ain Shams University in Cairo. In 2003, she received Human Rights Watch's highest honor for her work to end torture and promote women's rights in Egypt. *Cairo Review* Managing Editor Scott MacLeod interviewed Seif El-Dawla in Cairo on March 12, 2011.

CAIRO REVIEW: *What is the human rights factor in Egypt's revolution?*
AIDA SEIF EL-DAWLA: It was crucial. It was an essential component of the revolution. All this is about rights. It was triggered by the Khaled Said case [a young Egyptian killed in police custody in Alexandria in 2010], which was clearly a case of human rights violation, and death under torture. But it is also a culmination of long years of struggle for all kinds of rights: right to organization, to gathering, to democracy, to social and economic rights, to a minimum wage, to the right to strike. At the end, it's all about rights. The right to have a dignified life and to live a decent standard. And to decide who rules and by which terms. Every revolution is about rights.

CAIRO REVIEW: *This is something all Egyptians felt?*
AIDA SEIF EL-DAWLA: They might not know the human rights conventions inside and out. I don't either. But they know they were fighting, they were struggling, they lost their lives, because they wanted better life.

CAIRO REVIEW: *What part did the Khaled Said case play?*
AIDA SEIF EL-DAWLA: It mobilized many people against the issue of torture. Khaled Said was a middle-class young man. He did not belong to the population that is usually subject to torture—the poor, the marginalized. He was a middle-class young man who used the Internet and was a computer fan. He used the Internet café and

posted YouTube videos like so many young people. And I think many young people identified with him. I think his class played a role. The extreme courage of his family. And the identification of young people with him. And the fact it also took place so much in public. And the pictures that were taken by his brother. All these elements put together put him in the center of the campaign against torture.

CAIRO REVIEW: *Was it an extreme case?*
AIDA SEIF EL-DAWLA: No, it's the typical case. It happened so many times, in the previous regime, and in the current regime. We have been documenting cases of torture since January 25.

CAIRO REVIEW: *Is there a direct line between the Khaled Said case and the mobilization of people on January 25?*
AIDA SEIF EL-DAWLA: No, it's not a clear linear line, of course not. But it was a trigger. People went on the 25th on the Day of Police to defy police. And to reject police policies. What happened between the 25th and 28th was extreme stupidity and brutality by the regime. No one thought that the 25th was going to develop into what it developed into. There was severe brutality by the regime and it seems that the young people were really fed up. The way they challenged and actually ran against those tanks. And the way they picked up the tear gas canisters and threw them back. That was an angry young people. Who by the way didn't belong to anything. The political groups and the familiar faces and names, they all appeared in Tahrir Square on the 28th. The clash of the demonstrations after midnight on the 26th and 27th, those were angry young people.

CAIRO REVIEW: *Your memory of January 25?*
AIDA SEIF EL-DAWLA: There was the feeling that there is a defiance that I've not seen before. And a courage, incredible courage. And then at one point, it seemed that the security forces had given up for the day. Which happened before, on March 20, 2003, when demonstrations broke out [against] the invasion of Iraq. On March 20, people managed to take over the square. On March 21, it was a massacre. So this was also a concern. They were exhausted. People were coming from everywhere. And they'd retaliate the next day. Well, they retaliated the same night, and that was very brutal. The tear gas was incredible, people got shot.

CAIRO REVIEW: *What does the revolution say about the work of the civil society organizations over the years?*
AIDA SEIF EL-DAWLA: I think that everybody played a role. I'm not sure that civil society organizations played a major role. You can't pick and choose now, who said

what. Nadim, for example, started talking about torture in 1993. But it never had the impact. It had a major impact on the lives of individual torture survivors and their families, but it never had this major impact on its own. Except when the bloggers joined, before the Khaled Said case. Once bloggers got involved and started posting videos on the Internet, the whole issue took on a whole different dimension. I can't say, yes, civil society organizations contributed to the revolution. But everything before contributed to it. I can't overlook, for example, three years of daily worker's strikes on the streets, occupying the street outside parliament, etc. I can't decide what is it exactly. It's just the injustice became too much. The revolution, this process, has toppled the head of the regime. There's still a lot more to be toppled before we can talk about the success of the revolution.

CAIRO REVIEW: *People around the world, in China, Vietnam, other Arab countries, will be looking at Egypt for lessons as a model.*
AIDA SEIF EL-DAWLA: We're looking at Tunisia for lessons. Tunisia is far ahead of what we achieved. Their president left the country. Ours is still in the country, receiving royal treatment. Okay? They have dismantled the state security apparatus. They have dissolved the ruling party. They have toppled one government and are not letting go except when their agenda was achieved. We have a different situation. We have many people now who are telling strikers in Tahrir to stop, saying "What else do you want?" And those people aren't just thugs. The violent aspect of it is to a great extent thugs. But these are politicized people, people whose agendas stop at the constitution, elections, etc. It's funny. A call for the Khaled Said situation provokes the 25th. Now, with all this torture going on, also taken on video, also the victims themselves testifying, nobody wants to hear it. So we still have a very long way to go.

CAIRO REVIEW: *What is the situation now?*
AIDA SEIF EL-DAWLA: You have one hundred and seventy people now in detention, receiving military trials, right now, right now, as we're talking. And the lawyers there, they have no access to detainees, they don't have access to the interrogations, they don't have access to the trials. And those people may receive very harsh sentences.

CAIRO REVIEW: *Why is Tunisia ahead?*
AIDA SEIF EL-DAWLA: I think because they have a different leadership. This revolution [in Egypt] did not have a leadership. At least not a clear one. I'm not interested in who was leading behind doors. What matters is who is leading in the square. Tunisia after a while had a leadership: the Tunisian trade union, which is very strong. And they have relatively strong political groups. In Egypt, the situation was different.

The leadership developed after the revolution started. People kind of self-appointed themselves as leaders or as negotiators or whatever. And always creating a lot of debate. Not always happy debate, regarding "who are you to represent us," and stuff like that. For example, one coalition last week called [for] the ending of the sit-in in Tahrir. Who are you to decide whether the sit-in should end or not end? Who elected you? That's a major difference. Also, the size of the country and the strength of the state is different. [Tunisian President Zine El-Abidine] Ben Ali was a tyrant, but so far as a Mafioso can be a tyrant. But Mubarak was heading a very powerful state.

CAIRO REVIEW: *What was the role of human rights groups in the protests?*
AIDA SEIF EL-DAWLA: Our center is part of a coalition of organizations called the Front for the Defense of Egyptian Protestors. It was set up in 2006 to deal with demonstrations. They'd happen and people would get arrested. The lawyers would go to attend the interrogations. Another group would collect clothes and money and food and take it to the prison. It was all things that wouldn't last longer than three or four days. But, this [revolution], we weren't used to this. So as individuals, not part of organizations, we were in the demonstrations every day. My colleague and I actually stayed at the center for eighteen days because we received injured people. Our doctors went for a few days to the field hospital. We provided medicines. We transferred patients from the field hospitals to other hospitals when that was needed. Since things are quieter, we're documenting. We're receiving injured people and trying ways to treat them because some of them need sophisticated interventions. We are documenting torture and detentions.

CAIRO REVIEW: *Can you review the human rights violations since January 25?*
AIDA SEIF EL-DAWLA: We have over six hundred and eighty people who died. The majority of them died with live bullets. We actually had a few people at the center who would come and bring the bullets as evidence that they had shot the injured. Thousands of injured. We're far from documenting all of them. There are at least two thousand who went to the field hospital. There are problems with hospitals because in many cases hospitals would not give reports of the actual cause of death or injury. And that needed several interventions by doctors and lawyers we know. And then the disappearances, the arrests.

CAIRO REVIEW: *What are the figures for disappearances?*
AIDA SEIF EL-DAWLA: The figure that we have, at our center, is two hundred. Some of those might turn out to be deceased. The family of one went to the morgue every single day. They were always told he is not here. Then suddenly they're asked

to go and identify a body with a face that had no features. So now they're going to do a DNA test which can exclude, but can't confirm. And that's frightening, considering that nobody sees the detainees. And there are stories of several collections of corpses with different stories on how and why they died. So anyway, it's scary. There's a lack of transparency and lack of information. The disappeared are one thing. And those in the court are different. We are, mind you, receiving the tip of the iceberg. And we are receiving Cairo complaints. What's happening in the governorates? We don't have the information on that.

CAIRO REVIEW: *What do you know about the the episode in Tahrir Square on February 2, when the horses and camels arrived?*
AIDA SEIF EL-DAWLA: Our relationship to that event as a human rights organization was documentation of the injured and dead. Who died and where are they? And trying to help the families of the dead get certificates from the hospitals, to get the real reason for their deaths. There were different scenarios to disperse from Tahrir. There was tear gas, and firing, and there was beating and snipers, and there was this farce of the camels and horses. And then there were rumors. We entered a very strong psychological war of stories and rumors. You never know what is right.

CAIRO REVIEW: *What is the evidence of the police and army using lethal force against the protestors?*
AIDA SEIF EL-DAWLA: It wasn't Libya, okay? The army did not turn its tanks against the people and shoot at the people. The soldiers in the tanks let people use spray paint to write, "Down with Mubarak" on the tanks. The people were very passionate about the army. This is something the dates back to a long history in Egypt, but we have to understand the army and generals are one thing. And the soldiers in the tanks are another. It's not the soldiers in the tanks who take the decisions. But it was the same army which on the 28th opened up and let the thugs come into Tahrir to beat up the protestors. It was also the army that flew those F-16s for two days over the demonstrators. Terrorizing. At one point they flew very low. You had extreme vibration in your ears and some people lost consciousness. People need to believe in something. And of course the army is also clever. For example, in the first or second statement by the army, the general salutes the martyrs. This melts the hearts of people. Nobody wants to hear now about the army torturing or arresting. There is this message that's being propagated that those are thugs arrested by the army, for our safety and security. Many of them are not thugs. And even if they are thugs, you don't torture thugs, you bring them to trial. They're protestors. And it's funny that those people are brought in front of military trials, while the

big shots of the previous regime, including Mubarak, who is the high commander of the army, gets interrogated by the normal civil prosecution, and don't even have to show up.

CAIRO REVIEW: *Why is this still happening in Egypt?*
AIDA SEIF EL-DAWLA: There is a strong counter-revolution and there is a regime that is trying to maintain itself in power. There is no 'after the revolution' yet. And anyone who has the power and presence and police stations are going to use them. If this is what they use to hold on to power.

CAIRO REVIEW: *When you say the regime, who do you mean?*
AIDA SEIF EL-DAWLA: That's a very good question. If I asked you before January 25, what would have been the answer? Mubarak is not the regime. He is one person. There is the regime, the old guard, the businessmen who are screaming the country is falling apart because of the strikes, that the economy is falling apart after the strikes. Who's ruling? I don't know. This is Mubarak's army. It's not a popular army. It's Mubarak's army.

CAIRO REVIEW: *How do you move forward?*
AIDA SEIF EL-DAWLA: As human rights activists, we have very clear demands. Apology, acknowledgement of torture, dissolution of the state security apparatus, people should be brought to justice. And then—only then—can we talk about reconciliation. But the state security apparatus is still there. The rest of the people, they want the minimum wage, they'll get the minimum wage. They want independent trade unions, and they'll get independent trade unions. That's what people struggled for.

CAIRO REVIEW: *Is there any meaningful dialogue between the revolution and the army?*
AIDA SEIF EL-DAWLA: No. Because the regime picks up who they talk to. There's the coalition of the youth. Can you imagine if you bring a young person and the high commander of the armed forces sits and talks with him or her as if they're buddies? Of course, it's very attractive. But none of those people are independent. Each of those people are representing something political. Be it [opposition figure Mohamed] ElBaradei, be it the National Association, be it the Muslim Brotherhood, be it El-Gabha. The regime is talking with the young people, it's a big lie. There have been calls on this coalition since the torture stories came out, to stop the negotiations until they stop the torture. Stop the negotiations until they release the detainees. Until two days ago, it didn't work.

CAIRO REVIEW: *You don't sound optimistic.*
AIDA SEIF EL-DAWLA: I'm worried. I don't think I was ever more worried in my life than I am now. Before, people were very aware of how the situation was. Maybe they felt helpless or weak, but they tried. They saw what was happening. Now people are so tired. And those eighteen days in Tahrir, those were so overwhelming, to the extent that this possibility of a savior in the form of the army, no one wants to question it. They have wiped away the graffiti of Tahrir. The things that should have been kept as reminders of the revolution. They removed the graffiti under the title "Let's clean our country."

CAIRO REVIEW: *Is holding the regime accountable important for the success of the revolution?*
AIDA SEIF EL-DAWLA: It's very important that people who did human rights abuses be held accountable and be brought to justice. The reason why torture was so widespread, why it became a policy, was that the regime could get away [with] the fact that those people were not accountable to anybody. The people that were released from state security, when state security would tell them we are the highest authority in the country, they were right. I'm not pessimistic but I'm worried. And I know it'll take long, but some people don't want it to take long. Some people are tired.

Region in Revolt

Veteran analyst Rami G. Khouri predicts that the historic change sweeping the Arab world will lead to a secular rather than Islamist political order

Rami G. Khouri is the director of the Issam Fares Institute for Public Policy and International Affairs at the American University of Beirut. A widely published commentator on Middle East affairs, he is the former executive editor of the Beirut *Daily Star* and former editor-in-chief of the *Jordan Times*. *Cairo Review* Managing Editor Scott MacLeod interviewed Khouri by telephone from Cairo on March 6, 2011.

CAIRO REVIEW: *What are we learning about the Arab world?*
RAMI G. KHOURI: Two important things. Acquiescence and facility are not potential traits of Arab publics. For two generations, almost from the 1960s to now, the Arab world has put up with being the only collectively nondemocratic region in the world. Not a single Arab country was a credible democracy. They had traits of democracy, but very small and intermittent ones. And by and large it was a top-heavy, nonaccountable region. So we learn now that this is not something ingrained, that the Arab people were not comfortable with this and finally rose up to change this. The second thing we've found is that the only serious mechanism for democratization is Arab public activism. It's not well-meaning foreign aid, not small groups of civil activists in our country, trying this or trying that. And it's certainly not manipulating the public systems from the top. It's the public taking to the streets and demanding to change from autocratic to democratic systems. It's the only way to bring about that desired change. You have one common denominator, which is really constitutional change so that power is actually vested in the consent of the governed. People want constitutional change, they want principals and structures and values of governance—the exercise of power to be defined by the people through representative and accountable and equitable systems of participation and governance.

CAIRO REVIEW: *What is irreversible? What are the uncertainties?*
RAMI G. KHOURI: The uncertainties are many. The durability of these changes.

Will there be short-term regressions? What kind of systems will emerge? Will they be defined by Western-style democracy, or democracy colored with Arabism, tribalism, or Islamism? Will there be a major strain of urban cosmopolitanism defining these democracies? Will there be provincial, simple, rudimentary democracies? Will there be centralized or diffused power? The balance between presidential power and parliamentary power? The role of the judiciary? The issue of secularism versus religiosity. Fundamental systems remain to be defined. There are all kinds of really important issues. And of course we haven't had a single ideological issue raised yet. No one is talking about Israel, the U.S., Iran, secularism, women, foreign policy, tax policy. Not a single ideology has been brought up. This will come. But this is something that will be defined in the future.

CAIRO REVIEW: *What's irreversible?*
RAMI G. KHOURI: The only thing we can say is irreversible is that Arab citizenries will not put up with top-heavy security-anchored governments. They'll resist these. How? That depends on the country. But it's clear that we have awoken a sleeping giant. This is akin to the civil rights movement in the United States. Mohammed Bouazizi in Tunisia is our Rosa Parks. He's that one person, for that one moment, who undertook one act of great defiance and anger and self-affirmation. It happened, tragically, to be self-immolation. But it's that one act that captured the agony and indignities of the several generations of his citizens and his people. That one act sparked a rather brutal response from the Tunisian regime, then spread to ignite a protest movement that forever would change the modern Arab world. Just as Rosa Parks in her one act of refusing to give up her seat on the bus in Montgomery brought about ten years later the Civil Rights Act, and the whole change in the political system of the United States. That will never be reversed in the United States. And the same is the situation in our case in the Arab world.

CAIRO REVIEW: *How dangerous is the situation, in terms of political instability, economic costs?*
RAMI G. KHOURI: Any major national political transformation has risks. If you go back to the overthrow of the Soviet empire, there were problems afterwards. There still are. There was suffering, there was inequity, there was abuse of power. You still have great power imbalances, abuse of power by small elites. There are clearly dangers in the process. People will be hurt. People will suffer. Some people will do better than others. If you take a country like Egypt, where you have enormous economic and population pressures, it's impossible for the Egyptian economy to quickly generate the kind of numbers of jobs that will resolve the problems of youth unemployment and widespread low income. You need to do that while you're reconfiguring and relegitimizing

your entire political governance system. That's a tall order. The people will put up with pressures and problems if they feel that the system they are creating takes away the old indignities and humiliations.

CAIRO REVIEW: *Such as?*
RAMI G. KHOURI: The two things still driving the revolt are material pressures and intangible indignities. The material pressures are income, jobs, clean water, equitable delivery of health services. The intangible indignities are abuse of power, corruption. You feel as an ordinary citizen you are mistreated by your own government, by your own police, you don't feel your voice counts or is even heard. People will put up with tangible pressures like jobs for the entire population if the intangible issues are resolved. If police are not mistreating people, if you go to a government office for a routine service and you are not treated like an animal.

CAIRO REVIEW: *Is the Arab world ready for democracy?*
RAMI G. KHOURI: There is no doubt that there is both the will and the logistical expertise available and the composure to be able to make the transition. You're seeing it already in places like Tunisia and Egypt. Where it's only been a couple of months but you can see this process unfold. Clearly the Arab world has both at home and among the immigrant community abroad all of the human expertise to do this. I think you're going to see tens of thousands of Arabs come back to the Arab world especially in places like Libya, Syria, Egypt, and Tunisia where people have left because they were dissatisfied with the political system and uncomfortable with the economic prospects. They gained tremendous expertise as bankers or engineers or scientists and also expertise in living as free citizens in democratic societies. This will be a tremendous injection of skilled managerial manpower and entrepreneurship and some money as well.

CAIRO REVIEW: *Do you expect broad changes in political orientation? Is this a victory for the Islamist parties ultimately?*
RAMI G. KHOURI: I don't expect radical changes. I expect some more limited changes. When the people start addressing ideologies and foreign policy issues, for example, you'll see a much stronger popular commitment to support the Palestinian people. I don't think the peace treaty with Israel will be abrogated. But people will say, we're at peace with Israel but we also support the Palestinians and will not allow Arab countries to be partners with Israel in the siege of Gaza or control of the West Bank. You'll see some changes in the rhetoric and you'll see some practical changes. You'll probably see a more clear and rational approach to dealing with Western powers, the U.S. and Europeans and others, demanding for instance that the Western powers be

less hypocritical, and practice double standards less frequently in their policies. You'll probably see greater understanding for the Iranian right to enrich uranium for peaceful purposes. You'll probably see a much stronger desire to cooperate with Turkey at a popular level. There will be a greater desire for people to cooperate and this will give birth to a new brand of pan-Arab cooperation and solidarity. It will be different from the rhetorical and emotional Arab nationalism of the fifties and sixties, but a European style of collaboration, integration, cooperation, and solidarity.

CAIRO REVIEW: *What about the Islamists?*
RAMI G. KHOURI: The Islamists will probably be the losers in the medium run. The Islamist movements, the Muslim Brothers and others, grew up in the last thirty or forty years and became the most important voice of political challenge. These movements developed because there was nobody else who was able do this. The government put everybody else in jail, or kicked them out of the country, or killed them, or emasculated them, or bought them off. The Muslim Brothers and the Islamist movements were the only ones that could keep working because governments couldn't close the mosques. These Islamist movements became powerful also because they were the most courageous people and they were the only people challenging the government and they went to jail and they were killed. So I think people will recognize the debt they have to the Islamists for upholding that spark of freedom and dignity. But [now] you have other alternatives: secular parties, tribal groups, professional business groups, democracy movements, human rights, women, student, labor, students, and other groups. I think the Islamist groups will go back to playing the role that religious parties play in most societies, which is they reflect a small number of committed people. I believe the Arab world will be a largely secular political world. You will have Islamism as a player, one actor on the stage. But you essentially have five forces that will have to find a balance among themselves in terms of political culture: Arabism, tribalism, Islamism, urban cosmopolitanism, and the state ideology, the nationalism. Those five identities will interact with each other. I don't think any one movement will dominate society as the Islamists have dominated the opposition groups to the Arab regimes. So I believe that the Islamists will get weaker not stronger.

CAIRO REVIEW: *How widespread will political changes become in the region?*
RAMI G. KHOURI: I think political change as such will be widespread, but it won't always be as radical as it was in Tunisia and Egypt. There will be demands for measurable practical change in the constitutions and in the governance systems and the exercise of power in countries. In Bahrain and Jordan, people are asking for constitutional monarchies. So the monarchies won't be abolished but there will be change. In other countries,

people want the old regimes thrown out, they don't want a single remnant of the old regimes. It will vary I think in every country but I think there will be change in every single country. Throughout the region people are discontented with the nature of the political system they live in. They want them to be more democratic, representative, and accountable. How that happens will depend on local forces. Some countries will have just minor but substantive changes that actually change something in the system that is enough to satisfy the citizens.

CAIRO REVIEW: *Why did this young generation revolt, and not the previous generation?*
RAMI G. KHOURI: What's different is the circumstances in which they found themselves living. The circumstances reflect the economic conditions, like population growth and job opportunities. Since the 1980s, the living standards have been declining. Parallel with that was the increasing police and security nature of the ruling regimes. Linked with that is the increasing unearned wealth of the ruling elite, the emergence of the kleptocracy in many Arab countries. And as citizens they are under increasing economic and social and environmental stress. On top of all that, they had to put up with continued defeats by Israel. Or finding themselves at peace with Israel even though they weren't at peace with Israel in their hearts because of what Israel was doing to the Palestinians and the Lebanese and others. And the humiliation of foreign armies, as in the Anglo–American invasion of Iraq. All these things together brought us to this moment in the last ten years when more and more people became angry. What happened with Mohammed Bouazizi's death was a widespread sense of indignity and anger and humiliation and didn't come out of a vacuum. People in different forms and different countries have been constantly expressing their complaints and challenging their governments and have never been able to break through the incredibly powerful mechanisms of the Arab police state until Tunisia.

CAIRO REVIEW: *People have credited Facebook as a tool for the revolutions, but how important were the satellite news channels?*
RAMI G. KHOURI: I think Al Jazeera was the single most important force here. If you asked me what were the most important communication channel or tools that were relevant to this whole movement and still are, it's Al Jazeera television, and cell phones. Others are the mosque and public spaces. In Cairo, if you wanted to get a message out, you just got it to the mosques and by word of mouth the message would get out in twenty-four hours to ten million people. I think we have to study this more carefully. There is no doubt that Facebook and YouTube and blogging and websites played a

catalytic role in some places. But the real digital factors mobilizing human beings were cell phones and Al Jazeera television.

CAIRO REVIEW: *Why different responses in different Arab countries?*
RAMI G. KHOURI: It's the nature of people's grievances [and] the nature of the political leadership. The way they subjugate people is different in every country. It's also about the degree of legitimacy of the ruling establishments. Some establishments like the Tunisian one and the Egyptian one were seen by their people to have zero legitimacy. That's not the case in every Arab country. That's certainly not the case in Saudi Arabia and Morocco, and Jordan, to an extent in Syria, and to some extent in Bahrain. So it's a combination of all those things, and partly the response of the regime. If the regimes are brutal, people might be less likely to go out and risk their lives. But that's the smallest factor, because we've seen pretty brutal responses in Tunisia and Egypt and now Libya and in Bahrain, and that increases the will of the people to get out there and change the system.

CAIRO REVIEW: *Why such a violent situation in Libya?*
RAMI G. KHOURI: I think that's largely a reflection of the nature of the regime. The Gadhafi regime is different. It also has to do with the structures that you have available to you. The role of the army in Egypt and Tunisia was critical in allowing the transition to happen quickly. The army ultimately went to the leaders and said, "The game is up, you have to leave. Your people no longer accept you. Spare them bloodshed and spare yourself." They were allowed to go and retire somewhere. They might be put on trial, we will see. In Libya, that's not the case. You don't have these institutions like the army that could mediate, that could go to Gadhafi and say, "The game's up." And the nature of his rule has been clear for forty-two years. This is an eccentric, oddball, violent man, and he's not hesitant to use violence against his own people. So partly it's personality-driven, and partly the structures of the ruling government systems that are in place.

CAIRO REVIEW: *Do you see a qualitative difference in the legitimacy of Arab republics versus Arab monarchies?*
RAMI G. KHOURI: My hunch is there is a little difference. Of course, republics over the years have become like monarchies trying to pass incumbency to their sons, and did so in some cases. Monarchies tend to be more sensitive to people's complaints. I don't know why that is. If it's in the nature of royalty, or simply they understand that because they are not elected, that people have to accept them, they have to actually earn their legitimacy by serving the people.

CAIRO REVIEW: *How is Jordan affected?*

RAMI G. KHOURI: The demands in Jordan are being expressed by a lot of people. It's fascinating, instead of saying "the people want to bring down the regime," in Jordan the phrase they are using is that they want to "reform the regime." They don't necessarily want to get rid of the monarchy and the king, but they want to change the way they exercise power. The king has made it clear that he understands this and is prepared to make some changes. He changed the prime minister and the cabinet but we'll see what difference that makes. He's done that many times without real change. Maybe things will be different this time. Clearly there is pressure on the king to change some aspects of how the governing system works. His problem is he keeps running into the Palestinian/Jordanian dichotomy. The Jordanians are always hesitant to open up the system, because there is a strong constituency of Trans-Jordanians, east bankers, who are fearful that if they really democratize the country, that the Palestinian-origin Jordanians, who are probably 60 percent, or something like that, would dominate the system. And that the Trans-Jordanians would lose some of their advantages, which they get because they are Trans-Jordanians. Perhaps this is the moment to get the Hashemite monarchy to go beyond that fear and truly open up the system in a serious way.

CAIRO REVIEW: *Are such regimes capable of reforming from within?*

RAMI G. KHOURI: Up to now, it's been obvious that they are incapable of meeting the demands. They've made superficial changes. They've talked a lot about reform, but not really done it. They only made very limited reforms, administrative reforms, increased efficiency of service delivery. They haven't done anything about the core exercise and accountability of power. They haven't been serious. But we are at a historic turning point. This is a completely new moment. You can't judge the years ahead on the basis of the previous years. The nature of citizen activism, the consequences of citizen activism, the nature of the demands being made, the public open nature of the calls for reform and change or to get rid of leaders, this is all unprecedented. This is a whole new ball game. I think we just have to wait and see if they can make the changes and stay in power or be thrown out, or in some cases make the changes and then later get eased out. You have cases in recent history, like Gorbachev in the Soviet Union, or F.W. de Klerk in South Africa, of leaders at the top who changed the system themselves. They saw that what they were living in was unsustainable and they took the initiative to change the system. And eventually it created better countries, more stable democratic countries, but they were pushed aside. It's possible that someone in the Arab world is a Gorbachev.

CAIRO REVIEW: *What about Syria?*
RAMI G. KHOURI: I think it has the same combination of popular grievances. People want change in different political and economic areas. The Syrians have the added dimension of the Arab–Israeli conflict. They claim they are leading the Arab struggle to demand that Israel withdraw from the occupied territories and give the Palestinians their rights, and that Syria leads the Arab side of the defiance and resistance front against Western hegemony. All these things resonate with a lot of people around the region. That probably has a grain of truth in it, but I think Syria at some point has to come to grips with the fact that the conditions that people are complaining about across the region are conditions that exist in Syria. They've shown signs of appreciating this. In the last year, they've talked at the top level about opening up civil society and have the private sector play a bigger role. But it's been very limited in terms of changing the core issue which comes up in every single one of these countries: real constitutional change that modifies how power is exercised.

CAIRO REVIEW: *Does the Syrian regime have more legitimacy because of its role in the Arab–Israeli conflict, or are they just better at state security control over their people?*
RAMI G. KHOURI: Security control isn't enough. The shah [of Iran] had pretty outstanding security control. Ben Ali and Mubarak had, like, nine-hundred thousand troops, or whatever it was. Security control doesn't give you perpetual control in itself. The people will rebel against strong governments. Each country has its own factors that define how it moves.

CAIRO REVIEW: *Are the Arab revolts affecting the prospects of greater democratization in Lebanon, which experienced the Cedar Revolution?*
RAMI G. KHOURI: What happened in 2005 is not the same as what's happening now. That was a movement by about half the country to push out what they saw as a foreign occupier, which was Syria. Now the question is whether the movement of change that's happening all over the Arab world will get into Lebanon. I don't think it will. If you look at the Lebanese system, it's a system in which every group in the country, every sectarian or religious group, eighteen of them, have official slices of the pie. They all have a share of parliament, generals in the army, ambassadors, senior bureaucratic positions. The system is designed in a way to institutionalize power sharing and divide up the assets of the state among the different confessional groups. Therefore, there is a huge difference between what's going on in Lebanon and what's going on in the rest of the Arab world. In other countries, citizens are challenging a strong state that they believe is illegitimate and denies their rights. In Lebanon, you have a weak

state, but that weak state is the vehicle through which citizens are actually empowered and have access to the resources of the state and its services and its jobs.

CAIRO REVIEW: *How do the changes affect the Israeli–Palestinian conflict?*
RAMI G. KHOURI: It's hard to tell. I think the only thing we can say right now is that a more democratic Arab world will naturally express more support for the Palestinian people. How is that expressed? Is it just rhetoric? Or is it security council votes, or sending aid? We just don't know. But definitely there will be more support for the Palestinian people, which will create more stress on Israel. There will probably be more clarity and diplomatic vigor in the Arab countries saying to Israel, "Okay, we put this peace treaty on the table in 2002. We're prepared to live with Israel as a predominantly Jewish state with a strong Arab minority. We're prepared to live with you in peace and accept you like Egypt and Jordan have done. Let's get off the fence and solve this conflict and Israel [must] do what it has to do to meet its obligations, end the refugee crisis, create a Palestinian state, and withdraw from the land it occupied in 1967." So you'll probably see this movement in Arab–Israeli negotiations. It might start unilaterally with Syrians, it's hard to tell. If this Arab democratic wave reaches Syria, and Syria changes substantially, this will have huge implications. A change in Syria will have implications for Hezbollah, Hamas, and Iran. So the geopolitics of the region will evolve in some form that we can't predict right now. I don't think it will lead to new wars. I think it will lead to intense new diplomatic and political pressures to end the conflict in equitable ways.

CAIRO REVIEW: *Is Israel capable of responding to a democratic voice from the Arab world?*
RAMI G. KHOURI: Under its present government, no. Israel is not capable of doing anything other than continued colonial oppression of the Palestinians in defiance of world legal norms. But the Israelis for fifty-five or sixty years have been saying that they are the only democracy in the region. If they are no longer the only democracy, that presumably should be a good thing for them. They presumably would welcome dealing with other democracies. I think they would. I think democracies would deal with each other in a more rational way. You'll have the possibility to end the Arab–Israeli conflict in the way, for example, that the Northern Ireland conflict was resolved, through a democratic negotiation through equal partners. With no pussyfooting around, but by being more clear, making tough, courageous decisions and concessions, but concessions that are done by both sides that each side gets their basic minimum rights. I think that's a possibility, but it's not going to happen under the present leadership.

FROM THE GUT

Decisions without Reflection

By Shibley Telhami

Decision Points. By George W. Bush. Crown Publishers, 2010. 512 pp.

A few months ago, I interviewed a prominent member of George W. Bush's cabinet for a forthcoming book on American diplomacy in the Middle East.* I focused a question about the influence and the apparent change over time of former Vice President Dick Cheney. This member of Bush's cabinet, who had worked closely with Cheney in more than one administration, disputed the idea that Cheney had changed over the years. What explains the seemingly different approaches that Cheney exhibited in the administrations of Bush and of his father, George H. W. Bush, he suggested, is above all else the differences between the two presidents. In other words, he said, I should be asking about George W. Bush, not Dick Cheney. *Decision Points* promised to shed desperately needed insight into the thought process of a man whose decisions affected world politics more than any other in the past decade.

Bush has penned a readable, thematically organized memoir covering issues ranging from the Katrina disaster to the financial crisis, which demonstrates the sort of traits that made him likable to so many Americans even as he was disliked, even despised, in other parts of the world. But the book is revealing in other ways that confirmed the worries many had about his decisions as the American commander in chief: there is an extraordinary absence of introspection on some of the most complex and challenging issues, and a portrayal of a decisiveness based on personal judgment.

One is left with the same impression that many analysts held during his years in office: Bush tends to make up his mind early, with only limited deliberation, usually based on instinct, and the hard work of the bureaucracies, the national discourse, the international consultations, was about selling and rationalizing what the president had already decided.

* The interview, conducted in Arlington, Va., was on the record but without attribution. It was part of the research for a book on American diplomacy toward the Arab–Israeli conflict, 1989–2009, co-authored with Daniel C. Kurtzer, Scott B. Lasensky, William B. Quandt, and Stephen L. Spiegel.

The trend starts with his decisions to appoint top advisors and his subsequent relationships with them. In his book, Bush reveals that after he won the Republican primaries the first time he ran for president in 2000, his first choice for a vice-presidential running mate, even before he put together a search and vetting committee, was Cheney, whom he had sounded out for the position only to be turned down. It was then that he turned to Cheney to head the search for a vice-presidential nominee. And despite a number of good candidates that Cheney presented to him, he dismissed most of them one by one. He came close to picking John Danforth, for whom he expressed nothing but admiration, before going back to his original choice. Cheney by then appeared more interested in the job, but worried that his health (and his gay daughter) could become political liabilities. Bush's key advisor, Karl Rove, originally opposed the idea and presented some good arguments against it. Most prominently, he worried that "choosing Dad's defense secretary would make people question whether I am my own man" and that Cheney added little to the ticket politically. But Bush had clearly made up his mind.

Still, in much of the book, Bush appears mindful of how his relationship with his father is portrayed and how the prevalent view that Cheney ran the White House was an issue he had to grapple with, and he tries hard in the book to dispel it. On one occasion, Bush tells of asking his national security advisor to convey to the vice president his displeasure that Cheney had moved ahead of him in his public statements on Iraq. He also describes how he considered dropping Cheney from the ticket in 2004, at Cheney's suggestion, as there was a sense that Cheney had become a political liability—and also as a way of dispelling the conventional wisdom that Cheney, not Bush, was running the White House.

The influence of 'Dad' is ever present in *Decision Points*, sometimes directly, sometimes in subtle ways. Even as he sought to differentiate his administration from that of his father's, Bush often sought his father's advice and backing. When he decided to choose Cheney as a running mate, his father's approval was sought and received. When he gave the orders to commence the war with Iraq, he sent a handwritten note informing his father, who wrote back movingly, "You carry the burden with strength and grace. . . . Remember Robin's words 'I love you more than the tongue can tell'"—a reference to a sister of the younger George Bush who died of leukemia. When Brent Scowcroft, the respected former national security advisor to Bush Sr., wrote an Op-Ed in *The Wall Street Journal* opposing the Iraq war, Bush was angered not only by the fact that he went to the press rather than to Bush directly, but also by the fact that people assumed that Scowcroft was speaking for the president's father, which George W. Bush denied vehemently. He called his father to vent his anger at Scowcroft's article.

One of the more revealing chapters in the book concerns personnel decisions. What comes across is a tendency to make personal and highly instinctive decisions on critical appointments. He recounts that former British Prime Minister Margaret Thatcher told him she usually made up her mind about a man in ten seconds. "I didn't operate quite that fast," Bush writes, "but I've always been able to read people." Besides his early decision on Cheney, his selection of Condoleezza Rice, as his national security advisor, with whom he had spent some time during the campaign—having been introduced to her by his father—was also quick, giving no indication of a full assessment of alternative candidates. He reveals that the appointment of Donald Rumsfeld as defense secretary was suggested to him by Rice, and enthusiastically endorsed by Cheney who had worked for Rumsfeld in the Ford White House.

His treatment of his relationship with Colin Powell is most telling. Bush, who turned to Powell for his first major cabinet appointment, notes that "Colin was widely admired at home and had a huge presence around the world. I believed Colin could be the second coming of George Marshall, a soldier turned statesman." But by the time Powell decided to leave the administration, Bush remarked that Powell's decision "made it easy for me . . . I admired Colin, but it sometimes seemed like the State Department he led wasn't fully on board with my philosophy and policies." In between, he took a few shots at the decorated general. He recounts instructing Rice to tell Powell to correct a statement the latter had made to *The Washington Post* about North Korea, even as Powell was on his way to see the president at the White House. In another instance, he tells of Powell passing him a note before he made a speech after the September 11, 2001, attack, suggesting ways to avoid becoming emotional, only to have Bush announce to everyone present that "the secretary of state just told me . . . 'Dear Mr. President: Don't break down!'" Referring to another occasion when Bush and his advisors heard what turned out to be a false alarm about possible exposure of the White House to a highly poisonous toxin, Bush writes that "Colin asked, 'What's the time of exposure?' Was he doing the mental math, trying to figure out how long it had been since he was last in the White House?" In a final jab at the man who remained more popular than the president throughout the Bush administration, Bush tells that his advisors suggested after his reelection that Powell was having a change of heart about leaving his post—but the president clearly showed no interest in wooing him back.

On the core foreign policy issues following the 9/11 tragedy—the 'war on terrorism,' the Iraq war, the Palestinian–Israeli conflict—the story Bush tells is remarkably close to the rhetoric of the period. There is a puzzling absence of discussion of the internal debate or even a full assessment of consequences, with selective memory only partially explained by the organization of the book, which is not chronological but issues-based. There is a glaring absence of lessons learned, of reflection on mistakes, which could inform future presidents. One is left with the conclusion that Bush believed almost all that he said while president.

His thoughts and decisions on how to deal with terrorist threats provided a clear example of his consistent positions now and then—and the basis of these decisions: "There is no textbook on how to steady a nation rattled by a faceless enemy. I relied on instincts and background." So he announced "a major decision I had made: The United States would consider any nation that harbored terrorists to be responsible for the acts of those terrorists. This new doctrine overturned the approach of the past, which treated terrorist groups as distinct from their sponsors." And yet Bush gives no indication of what sort of thought process he followed in pursuing what he believed was a radical change in policy, or any sense of the internal debates about the issue. We know, for example, that the U.S. Department of State had favored confronting terrorist groups 'with global reach' instead of a broader 'war on terrorism.' And when Bush gives an example of reservations put forth by former Senate Democratic Majority Leader Tom Daschle, the example only serves to suggest that Bush's decision was again based on instinct and personal judgment: "Daschle . . . issued one cautionary note. He said I should be careful about the word war because it had such powerful implications. I listened to his concerns, but I disagreed. If four coordinated attacks by a terrorist network that had pledged to kill as many Americans as possible was not an act of war, then what was it? A breach of diplomatic protocol?"

It is also clear that 9/11 and Bush's formulation of the 'war on terrorism' colored his approach to the Palestinian–Israeli conflict. To begin with, Bush accepted conventional wisdom about the failure of the Camp David negotiations a few months before he took office: Palestinian leader Yasser Arafat was to blame. And he saw Israel as a democratic state that exists within vulnerable boundaries that he had been shown from a helicopter by Ariel Sharon even prior to becoming president. Before he held his first cabinet meeting after the 9/11 attack, he had a phone call with Sharon, who had become prime minister, "a leader who understood what it meant to fight terror." But his biggest break with Arafat came in January 2002, when the Israeli navy intercepted a ship called the Karine A in the Red Sea with an arsenal of deadly weapons on board. While Arafat denied involvement, Bush says that the United States had information proving otherwise. That marked the end of the relationship with Arafat.

In a telling episode, Bush decided to give a speech that simultaneously favored the establishment of a Palestinian state (which was opposed by Cheney and Rumsfeld), and also called for a change of Palestinian leadership (which was opposed by Powell). Only Rice and her deputy, Stephen Hadley, supported the idea of the speech. But the headlines after the speech predictably highlighted Bush's call for replacing Arafat—so much so, Bush writes, that the president's mother called to rib him: "'How's the first Jewish president doing?' she asked. I had a funny feeling she disagreed with my policy."

These details were largely known about Bush's position and very much coincided with the public approach he took at the time. But on two key relationships for the president in the Middle East—with Sharon, and with then Crown Prince Abdullah bin Abdulaziz Al-Saud of Saudi Arabia–we get one-dimensional accounts that fail to describe the complexity of dealing with either. With the former, Bush describes an episode where he failed to restrain Sharon, but offers little comment; and with the latter he suggests that he was able to defuse the anger of the Saudi crown prince at Bush's failure to restrain Sharon simply by taking him for a ride on his farm, as if substance was simply a side story.

The remarkable story is that of the Iraq war. There is little indication here of any serious sense of failure or partial remorse, even with regard to the U.S. failure to discover weapons of mass destruction—a principal justification for the invasion—after the toppling of Iraqi leader Saddam Hussein. One certainly cannot expect Bush to embrace the world view of those who opposed the war or even to accept the prevailing conclusion that the war was unnecessary and the outcome troubling, at least in terms of the costs (both for Iraq and for the United States), the empowerment of Iran, and the failure to spread democracy. But one does expect more evidence of deliberation over painful choices and trade-offs, more insight into the failure of intelligence—and in some instances the doctoring of intelligence—and more reflection on the lessons for future decision makers. Instead we have mere repetition of the types of argument that the Bush administration had made before, most of which focused on Saddam himself.

"[Initially]. . . my policy focused on tightening the sanctions... Then 9/11 hit, and we had to take a fresh look at every threat in the world. There were state sponsors of terror . . . Saddam Hussein didn't just sympathize with terrorists. He had paid the families of Palestinian suicide bombers and given sanctuary to terrorists . . . Saddam Hussein didn't just pursue weapons of mass destruction. He had used them." The fact that it was Al-Qaeda, not a Palestinian group, that attacked American soil, and that this terrorist organization did not exist in Iraq before the war, but established a base there after the war, is not part of the story Bush tells.

The president's decision seemed simple enough: "We cannot allow weapons of mass destruction to fall into the hands of terrorists. I will not allow that to happen." In this view one cannot wait for evidence of the full danger: "The lesson of 9/11 was that if we waited for a danger to fully materialize, we would have waited too long. I reached a decision: We would confront the threat from Iraq, one way or another." For Bush, it is as if these are self-evident axioms that require no debate.

One can speak of the role of neoconservatives, of Cheney and Rumsfeld, of the many staffers who clearly helped make the case for the war, but in the end it was about a president who operated first and foremost on the basis of instinct and who was clear in his own mind about what he wanted to do. This is not to underestimate the influence of many of his advisors, including the neoconservatives who were particularly strong advocates of war with Iraq even before 9/11. But I have always believed that the decision to go to war was Bush's own instinct, not a product of the lobbying of neoconservatives, and that the power of this group, inside and out of government, was merely enhanced by its support for a president whose own instinct was to go to war. Once the president made up his own mind, neoconservatives became his biggest allies inside government and in the public discourse—and in that role, their overall power in the Bush administration expanded. Still, the manipulation of the information within the system, as well as its reinforcement of the president's own views, was undoubtedly a factor in encouraging the president to go all the way.

In the end, *Decision Points* is a frustrating, somewhat depressing book—and not because it is unclear; it is accessible and occasionally humorous. But one is left with the same judgment that one started with: either Bush is simply telling a political story that plays well to a public which had turned against him by the time he left office—with some success, given how briskly the book is selling—or he is as unreflective as he comes across. For those of us who understood from the outset that American presidents make a big difference in the conduct of foreign policy, particularly in time of national crises, and that George W. Bush became super-empowered by the tragedy of 9/11, when his own instincts and judgments were central to the critical policies his administration pursued for the next seven years, there was hope that the book would shed some light on the thinking of a man whose ideas and decisions were surely more complex than the sloganeering of his administration. In this book, George W. Bush tells us that what you saw and heard is really what you got.

How to Run the World: Charting a Course to the Next Renaissance. By Parag Khanna. Random House, 2011. 272 pp.

World Rule: Accountability, Legitimacy, and the Design of Global Governance. By Jonathan G. S. Koppell. University of Chicago Press, 2010. 392 pp.

The Future of Power. By Joseph S. Nye, Jr. Public Affairs, 2011. 320 pp.

The End of Arrogance: America in the Global Competition of Ideas. By Steven Weber and Bruce W. Jentleson. Harvard University Press, 2010. 224 pp.

In 1215, a group of rebellious English barons confronted King John on the field of Runnymede and forced him to sign the Magna Carta. Thus began England's long transition from absolute sovereignty to power sharing and participatory governance. Today, we are approaching a second Runnymede. America, as powerful on the global level as was King John in medieval England, faces new challenges to its role as the last superpower.

This transition will see America's leadership give way to power sharing with the barons of Beijing, Brussels, and Brasilia, and even possibly with upstart non-governmental organizations (NGOs).What the new system will look like, how it will evolve, and whether the transition will be as comparatively peaceful as that ushered in at Runnymede, however, are questions that all excite considerable controversy. Will we see continued American superpower hegemony? Are we moving, however slowly, toward a formal world government, perhaps managed by evolved forms of the formal global governance organizations (GGOs)? Or will we develop a new model of governance wholly unlike the familiar unitary state model, perhaps a model in which coalitions of NGOs, corporations, and individuals will increasingly manage issues directly, circumventing or even replacing states?

The authors of four new books on global governance agree that change is coming, and that the U.S. would be better advised to understand and try to shape the transition, than to oppose it. Even when arguing that America will or should remain the last superpower, they accept that more power sharing is inevitable. The question is how much and with whom.

Joseph S. Nye, Jr., frames the coming change as involving a dual transition. The first shift will see U.S. dominance give way to a new distribution of power shared more broadly with Europe, Japan, the BRICs (Brazil, Russia, India, and China), and others. The second will diffuse power away from formal states altogether and toward non-state actors, both intergovernmental and nongovernmental.

He argues that none of these newly powerful forces will replace America as the leading superpower in the coming decades. China's power will continue to rise, but China cannot take the lead globally without barons willing to follow it. Would Europe, Japan, or the BRICs want to see China supplant U.S. global leadership? Clearly not. Even if China were to become America's equal in economic and political power, the barons' backing for the U.S. would tip the balance.

Nye draws on his long career in foreign policy to integrate current events and historical perspectives into an insightful discussion of how the major global powers will benefit or lose from the dual transition underway. He cites the history of wars flowing from earlier transitions from one dominant power to another and points to several dangers inherent in the current double power transition. Even though the U.S. is likely to retain its leadership position overall, the U.S. must work to reshape its leadership style from one of presumptive dominance toward one of "preponderance," where the U.S. can "influence but not control" others.

Nye argues that, like Rome, the U.S. may face the greatest challenge to its leadership from domestic factors. Its outdated governance structure, designed to delay action and spread authority, may not be able to cope with the urgent need to modernize its economy and social services or meet global challenges. The coming decades demand unity and decisiveness, not attributes currently on display in American politics. He advocates a smart-power redeployment of U.S. leadership resources, one that will require the U.S. to step up to the "responsibility ... to produce global public or common goods" and to develop "smart strategies for power with rather than merely over other nations."

Steven Weber and Bruce W. Jentleson mirror Nye's advocacy of U.S. leadership through soft power. They openly call on America's leaders to frame policies that will regain American leadership in the "global competition of ideas." America must define a new, twenty-first-century consensus to replace the "five big ideas" that shaped global affairs in the twentieth century, which are that peace, benign hegemony, capitalism, democracy, and Western culture are each inherently superior to their respective alternatives of war, a balance of power, socialism, dictatorship, and non-Western culture, and will ultimately win the day.

These five big ideas no longer find acceptance among the majority of humanity living outside Western democracies, however. As Weber and Jentleson write, "the global population does not see itself as having benefited meaningfully from an era of American-led globalization." The rise of China and the U.S.'s mishandling of key engagements with the developing world, from Iraq to retrovirals, have opened the door to a competing "Beijing Consensus" embracing autocratic governance, a "market–Leninist" economy, the reaffirmation of communal over individualistic values, and strict limits to outside intervention in states' internal affairs. In short, broad prosperity trumps political freedom: "one man one vote" has become "one man one cell phone."

Weber and Jentleson also see danger in the coming transition, as the increased vulnerability of the global economy and environment to system disruption poses a "potent threat in part because the systems on which the world depends are now so tightly stretched." Rather than denying or opposing needed responses, an America determined to maintain its leadership must demonstrate that it can "make the systems we and others depend on more resilient and robust." It must embrace "mutuality" and reject unilateralism and American exceptionalism.

Like King John, the authors have ignored the barons' role in financing this new sovereign activism. The barons at Runnymede did not oppose King John's wars so much as the taxes needed to pay for them. Can we expect China to contribute to financing American investments at home and rebuilding of its influence abroad without also demanding a greater share in decision making?

Parag Khanna writes about the emergence of what he terms "mega-diplomacy," the expansion of nonprofits, corporations, informal coalitions, and even individuals into roles previously the sole preserve of nation-states. In his wide-ranging review of these developments, the single most valuable contribution is his analysis of how non-state actors interact with weak and failed states, and whether NGOs can fill the gaps, notably in human rights. He points to implementation challenges that impede this model, noting that "everyone wants to be the coordinator, no one the coordinatee."

In Khanna's new world of mega-diplomacy, success demands three attributes: inclusiveness to mobilize state and non-state actors for the achievement of shared global objectives; decentralization to allocate implementation responsibility to empowered and resilient coalitions of local organizations, not to ossified formal bureaucracies; and accountability to build "communities of trust" and mutual obligation among the participants to advance the mission. Khanna describes a world that remains far from achieving these three requisites, however. In Africa and elsewhere, weak and failed states have ceded power to non-state actors in a "new colonialism" of global NGOs and corporations—the latter increasingly Chinese.

Who, then, will run this newly decentralized and inclusive world? Khanna makes the case that no intergovernmental body, not even the G-20, will emerge as the new global governing council. Davos's World Economic Forum lays a stronger claim to being a global proto-parliament, where major corporate CEOs and charismatic NGO leaders meet with heads of state to set the global agenda and launch world-changing initiatives. In this new reality, the U.S. remains a powerful force not because of its military might but because "no other country has such a deep pool of resources outside of its government to beneficially shape the world."

Where Khanna captures the diversity of corporate, nonprofit, and individual actors engaged in mega-diplomacy, Jonathan G. S. Koppell takes a rigorously analytic look at a key subset, the GGOs that set and enforce global rules. He explores how GGOs actually get things done, the challenges they face, and the strategies developed in response. This is an important work, advancing our understanding of global governance and offering insight into whether international institutions are up to the task, are able to set and enforce rules on countries and corporations, and in doing so, can maintain legitimacy and accountability.

His rigorous and painstaking analysis of twenty-five GGOs provides, if not answers to these questions, at least solid evidence to advance the debate beyond rhetoric and speculation. His choice to focus on institutions working in diverse sectors and with established track records in rulemaking and enforcement lends force to his conclusions, as does his inclusion of intergovernmental, wholly private, and mixed public–private entities.

The crux of his argument is that GGOs face a built-in dilemma between authority and legitimacy and must adopt specific structures and strategies to overcome this weakness. In order to promulgate rules that make a difference and are followed in practice, a GGO must have authority. It therefore needs the legitimacy that comes from having a wide membership base and the promulgation of rules that are widely accepted and obeyed.

No GGO has independent enforcement power, however. In most cases, countries or companies retain the option not to adopt a rule, or to withdraw from the organization altogether. Rules that are too burdensome thus drive members away or invite members to ignore them. Not all members are equal, moreover; rules that are adopted lose authority if the strongest members—particularly the United States—fail to follow them, but lose legitimacy if they are seen as dictated by America.

GGOs respond to this dilemma by developing a range of strategies that give major players, particularly the U.S. but also at times major corporations, a large role in developing the rules to be adopted. To retain legitimacy, the system then provides opportunities for the broader membership to weigh in, even if only at the end of the process. An alternative strategy, that of adopting lowest-common-denominator rules, would only undermine the GGO by making participation a waste of time and resources. GGOs thus find themselves constantly balancing authority against legitimacy in both rulemaking and rule enforcement.

One of Koppell's most important conclusions is that, whether a GGO is a formal interstate body (such as the International Labor Organization) or an NGO with a mixed corporate–NGO membership (such as the Forest Stewardship Council), it faces much the same set of challenges and is likely to adopt similar strategies to overcome them.

Koppell stops short of offering a bottom-line answer as to whether global governance organizations are up to handling the urgent challenges of a globalized world. Are GGOs confined to relatively narrow action on specific issues, such as accounting rules or Internet numbering? Does the continuing failure of the World Trade Organization's Doha Round signal that even the most powerful GGOs cannot forge a consensus between the West and the rest when it matters? If GGOs cannot advance a positive-sum game such as trade liberalization, how can they tackle climate change, almost surely a negative-sum game in the short term at least? If we cannot create GGOs that work and are seen to be legitimate, then the feasible set of choices narrows to superpower dominance or chaos.

An intriguing leitmotif among these four works is the frequent comparison with another such period of chaos, the Middle Ages: like the present time an era of uncertainty and widespread conflict as one system gave way to another. As the four authors suggest, the focus now must be squarely on the major choices ahead of us and how we should think about them. Like King John and the barons at Runnymede, we know we cannot stay where we are, but we cannot yet say with any precision where the coming transition will take us.

◆ Jennifer Bremer

Aftershock: The Next Economy and America's Future. By Robert Reich. Alfred A. Knopf, 2011. 192 pp.

Robert Reich's new volume of popular economics is imaginative, engaging and clear-eyed—but one somehow expects more from it. The title alone, *Aftershock: The Next Economy and America's Future*, leads a reader to hope for some serious trembling: an 'aftershock', after all, evokes surprising tremors coming after a larger quake, it conjures the picture of already weakened edifices collapsing, and even the hope of creative destruction that accelerates the construction of something new. The larger quake Reich has in mind here is the great financial crisis of 2008. But this book is unfortunately not the story of an aftershock. It is not the tale of reverberations in an unstable system and how we might manage and control them. Instead it is a book that points at a fracture that still underlies American society—inequality—and then offers some well-known ideas about how best to close that dangerous gap. But the book is not courageous or aggressive enough in talking about how perilous this problem is, and how sadly limited our economic imagination for dealing with it has become. We need now an aftershock—perhaps several—and what Reich gives here is essentially little more than an afterwobble. It's not enough shaking, either for a book or for economics.

Reich begins by highlighting the link—what he calls a 'virtual pendulum'—that binds American politics and economics. The country, he notes, has historically swung from periods in which economic gains are centralized in the hands of a few to periods in which prosperity is widely spread. And while the immediate reasons for the pendulum's movements are economic, its real motor force is political. Policy choices lead to either distribution of wealth (as in the period after the Second World War) or historic and embarrassing levels of wealth concentration (see the last four decades). The aftershock Reich is now uneasily pondering is the snap-back of the political pendulum as a result of the excesses of concentration, which Reich believes is robbing the American economy of its vitality.

Reich's book then becomes a discussion of how a more equal society consumes more. He retells the stories we all know of negative real wage growth in recent years and an economy that has produced no new net jobs in over a decade. Until America's middle class is empowered—and employed—so that it can consume more, he sees no resolution to the have–have not economic conflict, and the inevitable emergence of a political fight as well.

What Reich proposes in *Aftershock* is a collection of sensible ideas to restore income equality: tax credits and other assistance for Americans earning less than $50,000 a year—the heart of the middle class—paid for by a combination of resource taxes and higher taxes on the wealthiest. Reich would tax the richest at 55 percent and eliminate most capital gains taxes—an attempt both to rebalance consumption and to balance out the absurd situation in which, as he explains, the very wealthiest Americans paid taxes at a 17 percent rate in 2009. He has in mind a world in which the market is allowed to breathe life into the economy, but in which the state helps press more people into that market on an equal basis.

Fundamentally, Reich is on to something powerful and important in understanding the way in which an unequal society—one of unequal opportunity and unequal security—will chew away at America's politics. He does a good job recounting the challenges to fundamental reform, but what he is missing is the sort of overarching idea that would make such substantial reform possible. He relies too much on the market in most places and doesn't ask the hard questions about ways in which markets are now failing. Reading Reich you're left with the sense of the need for a new economics. And you have as well a feel for the forces he sees devouring American politics: greed chewing away at the top, anger at the bottom. When the greed and anger meet, we can likely expect that shock he has in mind. But it's not likely to be an aftershock of the 2008 crisis so much as the first tremors of a much larger fault line, a shock that this book unfortunately tells us too little about how to manage, navigate, and survive with our values intact.

◆ Joshua Cooper Ramo

The Worst-Kept Secret: Israel's Bargain with the Bomb. By Avner Cohen. Columbia University Press, 2010. 416 pp.

Avner Cohen is consistent in an era of double standards and policy contradictions. In *The Worst-Kept Secret: Israel's Bargain with the Bomb*, he builds on his well-established works and commitment to the transparency of Israel's nuclear program. His arguments are often intriguing, and in some ways both philosophical and anthropological. It is correct that to have complete international and domestic accountability and effective control of nuclear programs, a significant level of transparency and a separation of powers between the nuclear regulators, the military top brass, and the political leadership is required. Cohen presents his case well.

Questionable, nonetheless, is Cohen's basic premise, which is that Israel would be better off with a declared nuclear weapons program than its present opaque, but not ambiguous, status. This is simply not true if the object is to enhance Israel's security. Cohen also argues that Israel should openly declare its nuclear weapons program in order to improve its international standing as a state that respects the norms governing the acquisition of nuclear weapons. It is very doubtful that this would in fact enhance Israel's political status because it would be upgrading its nuclear weapon posture more aggressively rather than contributing to nuclear disarmament. It is more likely that there would be severe repercussions, both regionally and internationally.

Cohen argues that having a transparent nuclear weapons program would enable Israel to overcome or counterbalance diplomatic problems it faces as the result of the stalemate in the Arab–Israeli peace process. There is no empirical or even anecdotal evidence for this. On the contrary, it would more probably reconfirm that Israel is pursuing renegade policies, inconsistent with international efforts to diminish the role of nuclear weapons.

Israel must seriously consider the ramifications of changing its posture from opaque and unambiguous to declared. It is difficult to make predictions, but regional states will be forced to react to the changing security paradigm and resulting political pressures, and react they will. Certainly, efforts to curtail nuclear proliferation in the Middle East—not to mention Iran—will become more complicated and difficult.

It is difficult to accept Cohen's argument for a change in Israel's nuclear posture. It is rather disappointing that someone arguing about enhanced security would ignore the fact that the asymmetry in nuclear programs and non-proliferation obligations has been a driving force for proliferation, thus determinately affecting international and regional security in the Middle East, including Israel. A nuclear weapons declaration by Israel would only fuel further such concerns, threatening the security of all states of the region.

Cohen's call for transparency is not misdirected, but it lacks context and comes at a bad time. Transparency would be a useful and imperative part of any steps taken by Israel to join the nuclear nonproliferation treaty as a nonnuclear-weapon state, like South Africa; or as part of the creation of a zone free of nuclear weapons in the Middle East that would include all the Arab countries, along with Israel and Iran. For transparency to provide enhanced security for all, including Israel, it should be coupled with a clear commitment to nuclear disarmament and the establishment of a nuclear free zone, with practical steps by Israel in that direction and a finite timeline for achieving that goal.

◆ Nabil Fahmy

Arab Voices: What They Are Saying to Us, and Why It Matters. By James Zogby. Palgrave Macmillan, 2010. 248 pp.

I couldn't resist making a cynical comment about U.S. public diplomacy when I testified before the U.S. Congress in 2004. As the George W. Bush administration launched wars in Afghanistan and then in Iraq, the State Department undertook aggressive efforts to improve America's image among Arabs and Muslims. Hired at one stage to lead the effort was Charlotte Beers, a successful Madison Avenue marketing executive. U.S. Secretary of State Colin Powell had quipped that she had convinced him to buy Uncle Ben's rice. "We are selling a product," Powell explained. "We need someone who can rebrand American foreign policy, rebrand diplomacy." Invited by a congressional subcommittee as the Al Jazeera bureau chief in Washington to comment on U.S. public diplomacy, I retorted in kind: "Marketing Uncle Ben's rice is different from marketing the policies of Uncle Sam's Rice"—an allusion to Condoleezza Rice, Bush's national security advisor at the time.

That is the same message in *Arab Voices: What They Are Saying to Us, and Why It Matters*, by James Zogby, who also happened to testify in that Capitol Hill hearing. The first part of the book deals with what Zogby calls "hearing problems," in which he emphasizes the need for the West to listen to Arabs themselves through public opinion surveys rather than stereotypes and anecdotes. Then, Zogby proceeds to detail and refute five "super myths" about Arabs, which he believes have been propagated by influential writers like Thomas Friedman, the "Foreign Affairs" columnist of *The New York Times*, and the late author Raphael Patai, author of *The Arab Mind*. According to Zogby, these myths are that Arabs "are all the same;" that they are disunited, driven by anger and religion, and immutable.

In making his case, Zogby, founder and president of the Arab American Institute in Washington, relies on his own personal observations in decades of visits to Arab countries. More importantly, he cites the findings of extensive surveys conducted throughout the region since 2002 by Zogby International, run by his brother John. Contrary to the claims of some pundits who emphasized Arab hatred, he writes, the poll data showed that majorities in all countries surveyed were favorably inclined toward American democracy, freedom, education, science, technology, films, television, and consumer products. "It wasn't American values or people that had caused the image of the United States to crater," Zogby explains. "America's overall ranking sank because of the incredibly low marks Arabs gave to U.S. policy toward Arab nations generally and Palestinians specifically."

In his final section, Zogby offers a blueprint for improving the hearing problems. His checklist includes: reaching out to Arabs in an honest dialogue; greater domestic transparency about the Middle East; progress toward resolving the Israeli–Palestinian conflict; demand-driven economic aid; more cultural exchanges; and utilizing Arab Americans in bridge building efforts.

No doubt that Zogby's stories, anecdotes, and polls reflect genuine Arab grievances toward the U.S. and other Western governments. Unfortunately, the book neglects to say much about the voices, either on the 'Arab street' or among Arab Americans, speaking out against undemocratic Arab governments. To what extent could we rely on public opinion in countries where most people didn't dare speak their mind? Whatever their good intentions, the pollsters may only be able to tell us half-truths.

◆ Hafez Al Mirazi